So You Wa

JOIN THE
MUSIC INDUSTRY

HERE'S THE INFO YOU NEED

Angela Erickson

SO YOU WANT TO . . . JOIN THE MUSIC INDUSTRY: HERE'S THE INFO YOU NEED

1405 SW 6th Avenue • Ocala, Florida 34471 • Phone 800-814-1132 • Fax 352-622-1875
Website: www.atlantic-pub.com • Email: sales@atlantic-pub.com
SAN Number: 268-1250

Library of Congress Cataloging-in-Publication Data

Names: Erickson, Angela.
Title: So you want to... join the music industry : here's the info you need / by: Angela Erickson.
Description: Ocala, Florida : Atlantic Publishing Group, [2017] | Includes bibliographical references and index.
Identifiers: LCCN 2016056090 (print) | LCCN 2016056913 (ebook) | ISBN 9781620232033 (alk. paper) | ISBN 1620232030 (alk. paper) | ISBN 9781620232040 (ebook)
Subjects: LCSH: Music trade—Vocational guidance.
Classification: LCC ML3795 .E75 2017 (print) | LCC ML3795 (ebook) | DDC 780.23—dc23
LC record available at https://lccn.loc.gov/2016056090

Printed in the United States

PROJECT MANAGER: Rebekah Sack • rsack@atlantic-pub.com
ASSISTANT EDITOR: Rebekah Slonim • rebekah.slonim@gmail.com
COVER DESIGN: Jackie Miller • millerjackiej@gmail.com
INTERIOR LAYOUT AND JACKET DESIGN: Nicole Sturk • nicolejonessturk@gmail.com

Reduce. Reuse.
RECYCLE.

A decade ago, Atlantic Publishing signed the Green Press Initiative. These guidelines promote environmentally friendly practices, such as using recycled stock and vegetable-based inks, avoiding waste, choosing energy-efficient resources, and promoting a no-pulping policy. We now use 100-percent recycled stock on all our books. The results: in one year, switching to post-consumer recycled stock saved 24 mature trees, 5,000 gallons of water, the equivalent of the total energy used for one home in a year, and the equivalent of the greenhouse gases from one car driven for a year.

Over the years, we have adopted a number of dogs from rescues and shelters. First there was Bear and after he passed, Ginger and Scout. Now, we have Kira, another rescue. They have brought immense joy and love not just into our lives, but into the lives of all who met them.

We want you to know a portion of the profits of this book will be donated in Bear, Ginger and Scout's memory to local animal shelters, parks, conservation organizations, and other individuals and nonprofit organizations in need of assistance.

– Douglas & Sherri Brown,
President & Vice-President of Atlantic Publishing

TABLE OF CONTENTS

INTRODUCTION

Quick—name your favorite song!

Now, that probably wasn't difficult to do; we all have our favorite songs to listen to or sing along with. Each of us has unique tastes—but we can all agree that music is a part of everyone's daily life, and it's also a huge part of our modern-day culture.

A lot of things happen to make a song or artist or record label successful. You will find that the process is more than writing songs, scoring No. 1 hits, and playing live venues. If you've ever been interested in discovering how your favorite song got on the radio, this is the resource for you. Plus, if you've ever wanted to be a part of that process, then you *definitely* want to read this book! Whatever your motivation, we will help you figure out every aspect of what it takes to be in the music industry. Here, you will discover all about record labels and music production as well as the different occupations involved.

First of all, we need to set some things straight. You may hear the word "record" and picture one of those big, black, circular things your parents (or grandparents!) played on a machine with a needle. If we say "record" in this book, it means any form in which music is recorded and sold—a vinyl record, CD, DVD, tape cassette, MP3 file, audio download, and any new technology that has not yet appeared in the market. The world of music is evolving so rapidly that it's pretty challenging to anticipate the next direction it will take. Trends in the music industry are driven not only by new technologies, such as cell phones with universal wireless access, but also by new forms of social networking and sharing music, such as Facebook®, YouTube®, Pandora®, and Spotify®.

♫ FAST FACT

When you hear a song you enjoy, your brain releases dopamine, a chemical in the brain that induces pleasure.

One huge aspect of the music industry is learning how to be flexible when things are changing so quickly. Laws about music and copyrights are changing. The ways musicians are being paid are changing. (Did you know hardly anyone makes huge amounts of money off of actual record sales anymore?)

Downloading and streaming music have changed a lot—but we'll get to that!

Recording an album is just the first step. The real challenge is getting that album out into the marketplace, building an image, and winning over the fans—plus making a living for all the producers and artists involved with the record. You will need a wide range of skills, including knowing good music, being able to work well with others, and understanding a little bit about marketing and distribution. If you are lacking in any of these areas, you need to find others with those skills who can partner with you.

As those who came before you can say, success doesn't happen overnight in the music industry. It can take years of extremely hard work to achieve anything resembling fame. If a life in music is your dream, be prepared for a rollercoaster ride. You will learn to make the most of the peaks and to strategize your way through the valleys. Every artist is different, and so is every record label. The more you know about the business in general, the greater are your chances of success.

So let's get started!

CHAPTER 1

Music Labels

Here you are! You're ready to explore and learn all about the music industry. We're going to begin with a big picture concept: music labels.

SO ... WHAT'S A MUSIC LABEL ANYWAY?

That's a great question! In a nutshell, a music label is an entity that produces and markets music. A label can be a single person working from a home office with a laptop, or it can be a corporation with a large advertising budget and a full-time staff of producers, talent agents, sound engineers, graphic artists, marketing professionals, and distributors.

WHAT'S AN INDEPENDENT MUSIC LABEL?

An independent music label or "indie" is just that—it is funded and operated independently from the major record labels that dominate mainstream music markets. Today, some independent labels collaborate with major record labels in distribution or production deals. Over the years, many independent labels have been purchased by major record labels seeking to expand into new markets. In some cases, these labels have kept artistic control and maintained their unique images while receiving support from the parent label.

WHO ARE THE "BIG THREE"?

Three major record labels, known as The Big Three, represent as much as 75 percent of the annual music market. They are Warner Music Group, Universal Music Group, and Sony Music Holdings Inc. An artist may be contacted directly to the major label or to one of its subsidiaries. Subsidiary labels are typically made by the major label that owns them. In some cases, major labels offer distribution services with their own markets.

Ready for a little history? Here's how the Big Three came to be:

Warner Music Group

One of the most famous recording labels didn't start because of passion for and excitement about music. It was formed in order to divert money from competitors.

Warner Bros., a movie and television studio, started Warner Bros. Records in 1958 to release its movie soundtracks after one of its actors, Tab Hunter, scored a hit with "Young Love" for Dot Records, a subsidiary of rival Paramount Pictures. Rock 'n' roll and pop music was just taking off, and the label was soon a major entity in its own right.

Over the next decade and following, Warner Bros. switched hands and focus many times, with an overall trend toward including more and more types of music and making more and more money.

♫ FAST FACT

WEA (an earlier name for Warner Music Group) jump-started the U.S. careers of Madonna, Ice-T, Depeche Mode, Echo & the Bunnymen, The Pretenders, and The Cure, and later successfully promoted Seal, k.d. lang, Tommy Page, and Ministry. WEA labels also signed contracts with The Cars and Prince.

Remember: Even if you don't recognize all (or many) of the names in the following lists, getting a sense of the size and scope of these labels is the important part. And if you're interested in the music industry, you probably want to acquaint yourself with many of these artists — both their music and their stories. You could ask your parents (or grandparents) for their recommendations from the 1960s and 1970s artists.

1960s

1963   Warner Bros. Records purchases Frank Sinatra's label, Reprise Records

1968   Seven Arts Productions buys Warner Bros. and acquires Atlantic Records, a dominant jazz and R&B label

Acquires rights to Atlantic's rock artists, including:

- Led Zeppelin
- Cream
- Crosby Stills & Nash
- Yes
- Average White Band
- Dr. John
- King Crimson
- Bette Midler
- Foreigner

Also acquires rights to the music of many soul and blues recordings

1969   Kinney National Services purchases Warner-Seven Arts for $400 million

1970s

1970   Kinney pays $10 million for Elektra and its sister company, Nonesuch Records

From the purchase of Elektra, acquires rights to:

- Rich variety of folk, classical, and world music
- The Doors

- Judy Collins
- The Stooges
- And more

1971 The company changes its name to Warner Communications, but is known in the music community as WEA (Warner Elektra Atlantic), reflecting three of its main sources

1972 WEA acquires Asylum Records

This brings in the work of many artists, such as:

- Linda Ronstadt
- The Eagles
- Jackson Browne
- Joni Mitchell

1977 WEA becomes the distributor for several punk rock and new wave bands, including:

- Ramones
- The Dead Boys
- Talking Heads

1980s

1981-1984 Warner Communications is a partner in the launch of MTV

1988 WEA acquires the German classical label Teldec and the British record label Magnet Records

1989 WEA buys CGD Records, based in Italy, and MMG Records, based in Japan

1990s

1990 Warner Communications merges with Time Life to create Time Warner Cable, the largest media company in the world at that time, and purchases the French label Carrere Disques

1991 WEA is renamed Warner Music

1992 Warner Music acquires the French classical label Erato, and acquires a 50 percent stake in Rhino Records

1993 Warner Music acquires DRO Group, a Spanish label; Magneoton, a Hungarian label; Telegram Records, a Swedish label; Continental Records, a Brazilian label; and Fazer Musiiki, a Finnish label

1996 Time Warner takes over Turner Broadcasting System

1998 Time Warner completely owns Rhino Records, which it had gradually been acquiring

2000s

2000 Time Warner consolidates with AOL but suffers reverses when the dot-com bubble bursts

2004 Time Warner sells Warner Music Group (WMG) to a group of investors led by Edgar Bronfman Jr. for $2.6 billion

2009 WMG acquires Rykodisc and Roadrunner Records

2008 WMG's Atlantic Records reports that 51 percent of its revenue from music sales in the U.S. comes from digital products

Mid-2010 Digital music makes up 30 percent of WMG's revenues worldwide and 47 percent of its U.S. revenues

Universal Music

Universal Music may not make the most music, but it sells the most.

Unlike Warner Music Group, its origins are in a talent agency formed to help musicians. But that agency, MCA Inc., didn't start out helping musicians sell music. It started by helping musicians figure out their schedules when they went on tours.

Universal Music is not the biggest record label, but according to the IFPI (International Federation of the Phonographic Industry) it is the top-selling label, thanks to its more than 100 subsidiaries. Universal Music originated as MCA Inc. (Music Corporation of America), a U.S. talent agency founded in 1924 that pioneered the practice of booking tours for musicians and entertainers.

1960s

1962   MCA merges with Decca Records, acquiring Universal Pictures in the process. At this time, Decca Records owns Coral Records and Brunswick Records

1966   MCA forms Uni Records in 1966

1967   MCA buys Kapp Records and begins releasing its music outside the U.S. as MCA Records

1970s

1971   MCA merges with Decca, Kapp, and Uni into MCA Records in California

1972   The first U.S. release from MCA Records is Elton John's "Crocodile Rock"

1973   Elton John's *Goodbye Yellow Brick Road* album and The Who's double album *Quadrophenia* are released by MCA in October; they vie for the top two positions on the U.S. *Billboard*'s Top 200 Albums chart for weeks

1977   MCA sets up its Infinity Records division in New York City to strengthen MCA's presence on the East Coast

1979   MCA acquires ABC Records along with its subsidiaries Paramount Records, Dunhill Records, Impulse! Records, Westminster Records, and Dot Records

1980s

1980   Infinity Records is fully absorbed into the parent company

1988   MCA acquires Motown Records

1989   MCA creates a new holding company called MCA Music Entertainment Group, which then acquires GRP Records and Geffen Records

1990s

1990   The MCA parent company is bought by the Matsushita group

1995   Seagram Company Ltd. acquires 80 percent of MCA and renames its music division Universal Music Group (UMG)

1997   MCA Records adopts a new logo, which highlights the parent company's former full name

1998   Seagram merges PolyGram (owner of British Decca) with its music holdings

2000s

2001 The French company Pernod Ricard buys Seagram's drinks business and sells its media holdings (including Universal) to Vivendi (now Vivendi SA)

2003 The UMG label Geffen Records absorbs MCA Records

2007 Vivendi purchases BMG Music Publishing for $2.4 billion and becomes the world's largest music publisher

Sony Music Holdings

Sony Music Holdings didn't start out as its own company and gradually become larger. It started out as the result of a merger.

Today, Sony Music Holdings is the second largest of the four major record labels and controls 25 percent of the music market. Sony originated from the American Record Company (ARC), formed in July 1929 by a merger of four smaller record companies.

♫ FAST FACT

Warner Music Group claimed the copyright of the "Happy Birthday" song until February 2016 — even though the song was probably made more than 100 years ago. They settled for $14 million to bring the song into the public domain.

1920s

1929   ARC is taken over by Consolidated Film Industries

1930s

1938   Columbia Broadcasting System (CBS) purchases ARC for $700,000. CBS made the American Columbia label its flagship (the U.K. Columbia label became successful under EMI Records)

1950s

1951   CBS arranges to distribute its music internationally through Philips Records

1953   CBS founds Epic Records

1958   CBS founded Date Records to market rockabilly music (later, in 1966, the label changed to soul music)

1960s

1967   CBS Records plunges into rock music, signing many artists, including:

- Janis Joplin with Big Brother & the Holding Company
- Laura Nyro
- Jimmie Spheeris
- Electric Flag
- Santana
- The Chambers Brothers
- Bruce Springsteen
- Andy Pratt
- Chicago

- Billy Joel
- Blood, Sweat & Tears
- Pink Floyd

1968   CBS enters a joint venture in Japan with Sony: CBS/Sony Records

1970s

1970   CBS Records revives Embassy Records in the United Kingdom and Europe to release budget re-issues of albums that had originally been released in the U.S. under Columbia Records

1980s

1983   CBS begins releasing some of the first compact discs in the U.S. market, due to a joint venture with Sony

1987   The Sony Corporation of America purchases CBS Records for $2 billion in November

2000s

2004   Sony Music and Bertelsmann Music Group (BMG) merge to form Sony BMG Music Entertainment

2005   Sony BMG is fined $10 million after the New York Attorney General's office determined that it had been paying radio stations and disc jockeys to play the songs of various artists, an illegal practice known as payola

2008   Sony acquired Bertelsmann's 50 percent stake in Sony BMG and renames the company Sony Music Entertainment Inc. (SME)

Today, it is called Sony Music Holdings.

WAIT ... DIDN'T IT USED TO BE "THE BIG FOUR"?

Why, yes! There used to be four mega-labels, including the three mentioned already, *plus* EMI. What happened? It was actually bought out in 2012. Here's some background:

EMI Group (Electric & Musical Industries Ltd.), formed in 1931, was the fourth largest of the four major record labels. When the U.K. Columbia Graphophone Company and the Gramophone Company merged, the Gramophone Company's subsidiaries throughout the British Commonwealth continued to dominate the popular music industries in India, Australia, and New Zealand until the 1960s. The year it was founded, the company opened a recording studio at Abbey Road, London.

During the 1930s, legal issues forced EMI to sell Columbia USA; it retained the rights to the Columbia name elsewhere in the world until the Columbia name was retired in 1972. EMI wasn't a big part of the U.S. music scene until the 1950s.

1950s

1951   Columbia America cut ties with EMI.

1952   EMI releases its first long-playing records (LPs).

1955   EMI releases its first stereophonic recordings.

1957   EMI reenters the U.S. market when it buys 96 percent of the stock of Capitol Records.

1970s

1979   EMI Ltd. Merges with THORN Electrical Industries to form Thorn EMI.

1990s

1991   Thorn EMI acquires Chrysalis Records.

1992   Thorn EMI acquires Virgin Records in 1992, one of its most expensive acquisitions.

1996   Shareholders vote to separate Thorn Electrical Industries from EMI and name the new media company EMI Group PLC.

2000s

2000   EMI licenses its catalog in a digital format to Streamwaves, the first company to launch an internet subscription service with major label content.

2007   EMI announces a loss of almost $420 million for the previous fiscal year.

2010s

2010   EMI announces pre-tax losses of $2.82 billion due to debt, in spite of making a profit of $481 million during the previous fiscal year.

2011   Citigroup took ownership of EMI Group from Terra Firma and wrote off $3.5 billion of debt.

2012   After rejecting a takeover bid from Warner Bros., EMI was bought by Terra Firma, a private equity group. Some of its artists left the company because they doubted a private equity firm could adequately handle their affairs.

WHAT EXACTLY DOES A MAJOR RECORD LABEL DO?

Besides finding talent to perform and record songs, major labels spend lots of money to promote and market their artists. A label decides to sign an artist or band if the executives believe the artist can sell a decent amount of music. Once a contract is signed, hundreds of the label's employees work on producing, recording, releasing, and publicizing the artist's music. The label arranges radio play, publicity, concert tours, and distribution through its own well-established channels. In return, the artist must give up some aspects of his or her own career, and, in many cases, artistic freedom.

Each of the major labels has a music publishing arm that manages the rights to its artists' music and lyrics. The music publishing branch is an important source of revenue because it earns money every time someone wants to copy, perform, or re-release a song. Night club entertainers, high school glee clubs, orchestras, bands, and choirs all must pay to use the copyrighted music. Another important asset is the record label's catalog — the entire collection of every song ever sung by every artist or group. These past hits can be re-released as compilations, box sets, and commemorative albums. Many catalogs are acquired when a label is purchased by another label.

INDEPENDENT LABELS

Independent record labels have played an important role in introducing new forms of popular music to the world. After World War II, independent labels — specializing in jazz, country, folk, blues, and rock 'n' roll — catered to small but devoted audiences and gave artists the creative freedom to develop unique styles. Independent labels such as the Beatles' Apple Records, Rolling Stone Records, and Elton John's Rocket were founded by artists who wanted more control over their careers. Many of these labels later shut down or were absorbed by the major record labels, but some of them remain in business today.

♫ FAST FACT

At first, no record label would sign Jay-Z. So he started his own (**www.huffingtonpost.com**).

Each successful independent record label has a unique story, but all of them share some things in common.

- Their founders were passionate about music and were often musicians themselves.

- The founders were able to sign at least two or three artists who produced hit records.

- The founders learned by trial and error; they responded to each new challenge in creative ways that allowed them to keep growing.

- Many of the founders were young and knew little about business when they started, but they had a vision for their labels. Their flexibility and creativity allowed them to change with the times, quickly moving into digital music, streaming, internet downloads, and social media.

Here are the stories of a few independent labels:

Dischord Records

Ian MacKaye and Jeff Nelson founded Dischord Records in 1980 to release *Minor Disturbance* by their band, The Teen Idles. Dischord is a local label that supports punk rock music in the Washington, D.C., area. In addition to being a musician, MacKaye is a sound engineer and producer, and he is responsible for the exceptional quality of the label's early releases. The label is known for its strict do-it-yourself ethic; it produces all of its albums by itself and sells them at discount prices without the help of major distributors.

Epitaph Records

Epitaph Records was founded in 1981 by Bad Religion guitarist Brett Gurewitz to promote his band's albums. The label began as nothing more than "a logo and a P.O. box." It released a debut album in 1987 for the grunge band L7 and soon signed several punk bands, including NOFX, Pennywise, Down by Law, Coffin Break, The Offspring, Rancid, RKL, SNFU, Total Chaos, and Claw Hammer. Epitaph became widely known in 1994 when four of its bands (Bad Religion, which had left Epitaph by this time; NOFX; Rancid; and The Offspring) released hit records. From 1994 to 2001, Gurewitz left Bad Religion to run Epitaph full time. Epitaph continued to grow, and today it is one of the largest independent labels, active in the emo revival scene.

Merge Records

Merge Records was founded in 1989 by Laura Ballance and Mac Mc-Caughan to release music from their band Superchunk. The founders borrowed cash from their friends to finance projects. The label launched its first full-length CD in 1992. From 2000 to 2010, Merge releases by Arcade Fire, Spoon, and She & Him reached the top of the charts in the U.S. and the U.K. In 2010, when Touch and Go Records, the company that had handled Merge's releases since its beginning, announced that it would no longer manufacture and distribute records for independent labels, the company had to quickly find another distributor.

Naxos

Naxos Records was founded in 1987 by Klaus Heymann, a German-born resident of Hong Kong. Naxos is now the largest independent classical label in the world and one of the two top-selling classical music labels. In 2009, it began distributing streaming web radio and podcasts. During the 1980s, Naxos minimized recording costs by recording central and eastern European symphony orchestras, often with lesser-known conductors. In the 1990s, it began recording with British and American orchestras. Naxos focuses on making recordings of modern composers and little-known works of Japanese classical music, Jewish-American music, wind band music, film music, and early music. Naxos launched the online Naxos Music Library (**www.naxosmusiclibrary.com**), a paid service that allows subscribers to listen to more than 50,850 CD-length recordings from the catalogs of 320 independent labels. It offers access to librettos, musical scores, and artist biographies.

Orange Mountain

In 2001, Kurt Munkacsi founded Orange Mountain Music. This label's mission is to release some of the hundreds of hours of recordings made by

American composer Phillip Glass in the process of creating operas, film scores, musical theatre pieces, and records; performances of his solo, operatic, orchestral, and small ensemble work; and recordings by other artists and organizations that have collaborated with Philip Glass. Orange Mountain quickly established itself as a serious producer of quality music and soon began producing releases of new music as well as archival releases. By 2011, the label had produced 68 high-quality releases and continues to receive regular reviews in *The New York Times*, in *The Gramophone*, and in international music publications.

♫ FAST FACT

After Sony purchased CBS in 1987, CBS Corporation granted Sony a temporary license to use the CBS name until 1991 when Sony renamed the company Sony Music Entertainment (SME). CBS Associated was renamed Epic Associated, and Sony reintroduced the Columbia label after acquiring the international rights to the trademark from EMI. (In Japan, rights to the Columbia name belong to an unrelated company, Nippon Columbia.)

Rounder Records

University students Ken Irwin, Bill Nowlin, and Marian Leighton-Levy established Rounder Records in 1970 as a mail-order business to release recordings of blues, blues-rock, string band, and bluegrass music. Its catalog soon included folk, soul, soca (a modern form of calypso), Cajun, and Celtic music; at one point it also handled sales and distribution for as many as 450 other labels and had 100 employees. In 1985, Rounder was one of the first labels to produce CDs. Bluegrass artist Alison Krauss has chosen to remain with the label for the duration of her career, rejecting numerous offers from major labels. In 2004, the company launched Rounder Books.

In 2010, the label was acquired by the Concord Music Group, which does all of its distribution through Universal Media Group.

SST Records

SST Records was formed in 1978 in Long Beach, California, when Greg Ginn repurposed his mail-order electronics company, Solid State Transmitters, to release the music of his band, Black Flag (Panic). Ginn was frustrated because a label called Bomp! Records seemed to be dragging its feet about releasing a recording of his music. During the 1980s, SST released recordings by the Minutemen, Saccharine Trust, the Meat Puppets, Minneapolis hardcore group Hüsker Dü, as well as numerous other punk artists.

In 1987, the label decided to economize on promoting Black Flag albums by releasing them quickly, one after another, and supporting these releases with a heavy touring schedule.

SST released 80 titles in 1987 and apparently overextended itself, because several of its artists became dissatisfied with its services and signed with other record labels. In 1986, SST bought New Alliance, and it later created two sublabels—Cruz Records and a short-lived label, Issues Records, for spoken-word recordings. After being one of the dominant indies of the 1980s, the label lost prominence as Ginn gravitated toward jazz and many punk artists left the label.

Sub Pop Records

Sub Pop Records began as fanzine, *Subterranean Pop* or "Sub Pop," started by Bruce Pavitt and dedicated to underground bands in the northwestern U.S. In 1986, Pavitt and Jonathan Poneman created the Sub Pop label to release the EP (extended play—a recording that includes more than a single song but is not long enough to be an album and is often used to promote upcoming releases) of a friend's band, Soundgarden. In 1988, Sub Pop initiated a Singles Club, charging an annual $35 subscription fee and guaranteeing that members would receive a new single every month. The first single sent out was a single by Nirvana. As Nirvana's popularity sky-rocketed, Sub Pop became synonymous with the Seattle grunge music scene.

According to Sub Pop, its success was due to carefully orchestrated branding and unorthodox marketing. In addition to the Singles Club, Sub Pop created a uniform look and feel for its early releases. Its logo appeared everywhere—in its early days, Sub Pop sold more T-shirts bearing the Sub Pop logo than records. Sub Pop signed and promoted bands such as Tad, Dwarves, Mudhoney, Sleater-Kinney, The Postal Service, and Iron and Wine.

As punk moved into the mainstream music market, Sun Pop found itself competing with the major labels for artists. The cost of its aggressive promotions became prohibitive, and by 1991, the company was in financial difficulties. The staff was downsized from 25 to five. The company was saved by its share of the royalties on Nirvana's album *Nevermind*, though Nirvana had already moved to a major label. In 1995, Sub Pop signed a deal giving Warner Bros. 49 percent ownership, which has existed until the present. According to Poneman, the label made several mistakes after joining with Warner Bros: It opened satellite offices in Toronto and Boston, spent too much on band advances, restricted its policy for new artists, and established contracts with all its employees. Pavitt left the label in 1996.

The company, however, was well poised to take advantage of the shift to digital distribution and lower profit margins, with great success between 2001 and 2006. The company stopped paying oversized advances for bands and videos. Its bands are made as self-sufficient as possible, with tours intended to make money rather than be subsidized by the label. Realistic recording budgets give bands an opportunity to earn royalties even on modest sales. Sub Pop takes advantage of the opportunity for cheap promotion of new music through online channels. In 2007, Sub Pop launched the imprint Hardly Art under a new business model, in which bands own their master recordings and split profits with the label rather than receiving royalties. Contracts are made for one release at a time.

SO, HOW ARE MAJOR LABELS DIFFERENT FROM INDEPENDENT LABELS?

While each individual record label will be different from the next, certain things do set independent labels apart from major labels. The main difference is obvious: size. An independent label will be smaller, both in the number of people working on staff and also the number of artists or bands represented.

A major record label has the money, staff, and connections to bring a newly released CD to the mass market, placing it at the exact same time in retail outlets all over the country and getting extensive airplay on commercial radio stations, and booking international tours. Major labels add to their profits by mass-producing their CDs, DVDs, or vinyl records. They print their labels and posters for pennies each in overseas facilities and sell them with big markups. Shipping and distribution cost much less when you have a lot of records. Independent labels typically focus their marketing efforts on a particular region or group of loyal fans, and rely on direct contact with fans and creative marketing to sell their records.

HOW DO RECORD COMPANIES MAKE MONEY?

A record label makes money by selling the music of its artists—both by selling new releases and by the sales of old songs and albums, compilations, boxed sets, and memorial albums. Digital versions of music like MP3s may be the most recent method for selling music, but they only surpassed CD sales for the first time worldwide in 2014. It might sound hard to believe, but cassette tapes are still sold as well! As you will read in Chapter 5, vinyl records are making a comeback. CDs, tapes, and vinyl records are sold online and through specialty stores, entertainment retailers, discounters, and mass-marketers such as big-box chain stores. Online sales of CDs are made through online retailers such as Amazon.com; the websites of traditional retailers such as Barnes and Noble, Best Buy, and Walmart; and the websites of record labels, affiliates, and individual artists.

♫ FAST FACT

According to Spotify, a label or publisher earns $0.006 to $0.0084 per single sale or stream (**www.theguardian.com**).

Digital music is sold as individual tracks or whole albums, subscriptions, and streaming services. Music is increasingly sold as downloads on mobile devices through many different companies (ever heard of iTunes by chance?)—and as ringtones for cell phones.

Depending on the contract, record companies can earn royalties on music they have produced. A royalty basically means that money is earned every time a song or album is sold or played. However, different rules apply to the songwriters, artists, producers, and recording companies as to how much of each sale each person will get.

Finally, a record label can earn money when its name and logo are used on merchandise such as posters, T-shirts, musical instruments, pennants, and dolls. The label can also produce and sell merchandise associated with its music, such as books, clothing, and commemorative booklets—or it can sell memorabilia associated with its artists.

It's important to think about how the shift from physical records to digital music has affected the way money is made in the music industry. Illegal downloading and file sharing has cut into the profits of what is legally owed to those who created and distributed the music fairly. It is impossible to collect royalties when someone copies a song on a CD or flash drive and gives it to a friend. Record companies are trying all different kinds of ways to protect their creative property and make sure those who deserve to be paid aren't cheated. Merchandise sales, concert tickets, music subscriptions, paid streaming services, making money through selling advertising space, and even taking those to court who illegally pirate music are some of the ideas being explored today.

What's the "360" deal?

In the past, major record labels made a profit of $2.50 to $4.00 on the sale of each CD. Now that so many people download music instead, this has changed. Customers buy individual songs rather than whole albums, and the profit on the sale of a digital file is measured in pennies, not dollars. To make up for this, major record labels are increasingly signing 360 (or multiple rights) deals—which allow them to get part of the earnings from all of a band's activities.

Beyond record sales, the label gets some of the profit from concert ticket sales, merchandise sales, music publishing, endorsement deals, and any other use of the artist's brand or music. In return, the label commits itself to developing the band's career over the long term, finding new promotional opportunities, and devoting more of its resources to marketing the band's image. Major labels admit that, in the near future, most music downloads will probably be free and will serve mainly to increase the sales of event tickets and merchandise.

There are many opinions about this type of deal by artists and their record companies—positive and negative. A 360 deal can be help everybody if the contract is clear, and in cases where a relatively unknown artist will benefit from a major record label's expertise in ways the artist could not achieve otherwise—for example, when a band's music is particularly suited to money-making pop radio.

What's a license deal?

In a license deal, the artist owns the copyrights, and the record label licenses the right to make money on the music exclusively for a specific number of years (typically seven). After that, the artist gets the rights back to license the use of his or her music for TV commercials, movies, and re-releases. This type of deal might work well for artists who have already produced their own recordings and don't need a lot of creative guidance. The record label might not be as motivated to invest in the promotion of a new release because it will only benefit from it for a short period of time.

What's a net profit deal?

Many independent record companies now follow a "net profits" model. The contract gives the record label the right to make back all the costs of producing and promoting a record, including costs that are usually paid by the label under a traditional contract, such as manufacturing, distribution, and marketing. The artist and record company then share the remaining net profits on a 50/50 (or other percentage) basis. The means that the record company gets money back from investing in the record and doesn't expect to be paid from the band's other activities.

What's a manufacturing and distribution deal?

In a manufacturing and distribution deal, the record label handles only the manufacturing and distribution. The artist does everything else. This kind of deal works well for a record label that already has success in marketing and distributing albums in a particular genre of music. The label might not make as much money because the artist owns the rights to the album.

What does self-release mean?

Advanced recording equipment and software such as Pro Tools has made it possible to record music on a low budget. A band may be able to raise the money to make its own recordings and then keep ownership of the copyrights, paying a record label only for the distribution and promotion of the music.

TALES FROM THE INDUSTRY: M.C. Hammer

Thinking and Spending Big

M.C. Hammer, the first hip-hop artist to obtain diamond status for an album and a known innovator of pop rap, has always managed his own recording business. In the mid-1980s after a record deal fell through, Hammer decided he too would start a record label business. He borrowed a cool $20,000 each from former Oakland A's players Mike Davis and Dwayne Murphy to start Bust It Productions. He sold records from his car and basement and eventually founded the independent label Bustin' Records (later Oaktown Records). Throughout his career, he moved Oaktown from one label and distributor to another while collaborating with and mentoring other artists.

In 1987, the label released his debut album, *Feel My Power*, which sold more than 60,000 copies. Hammer also released the single "Ring 'Em," which, through relentless street marketing, became popular at San Francisco Bay Area dance clubs. Hammer stunned on stage with a troupe of dancers, musicians, and backup vocalists, catching the attention of a Capitol Records executive. Hammer signed a multi-album record deal with Capitol and received a $750,000 advance. A revised version of *Feel My Power* was re-issued as *Let's Get It Started* and sold two million copies. His next album, *Please Hammer, Don't Hurt 'Em* ranked number one for 21 weeks and has sold about 18 million records to date. Although criticized by rap fans for his sometimes repetitive lyrics and his clean-cut good boy image, Hammer navigated a successful career that included extensive touring in

Europe and Asia. In 1991, PepsiCo sponsored him, and PepsiCo International CEO Christopher A. Sinclair went on tour with him.

Unfortunately for Hammer, his success was matched by a lavish lifestyle that included a $12 million mansion in California and a payroll of 200 employees. The concert tour for his fourth album, Too Legit to Quit, had to be canceled midway because, though the album reached #5 on the charts, album sales could not support the expense of the elaborate stage show. The music video for the album included a number of celebrities and was one of the most expensive music videos ever produced. As his style of pop rap became less popular with fans, sales of later releases did not match the income from his earlier albums. In 1996, when Hammer declared bankruptcy, he had gone through $33 million in royalties and was $13 million in debt. His mansion sold for a tiny portion of its original price.

Hammer's financial difficulties didn't stop him from continuing to release successful albums and singles, making a foray into gospel music, and appearing in films and on television. Today, he lives much more modestly and applies his know-how and drive to developing a series of new business ventures including clothing lines (J Slick and Alchemist Clothing), iPad app development, and most recently, Alchemist Management, a company that manages and markets 22 martial arts fighters.

♫ FAST FACT

If you add up all the costs, from recording to marketing, making a hit song can cost $1 million (**npr.org**).

CHAPTER 2

Jobs in the Music Industry

There are many ways to hold a job in the industry that are fulfilling and exciting for music lovers. As we discuss some typical job positions you might find working in a record label, we'll go over what qualities you might need for these jobs, and their responsibilities. It's good to remember that most people in the music industry aren't making a steady, regular salary but get paid for each project by itself. Many might not even have one steady job at one company, but constantly need to look for new work opportunities. While we talk about the pay successful people in these jobs might be earning, keep in mind there is a huge range for every job.

ARTIST

> **Question:** *Who's performing the song?*
> **Answer:** *The artist.*

An artist can mean a single person, or an entire band. Making money depends on the popularity of the songs, and the details of the contract. Some artists struggle, while others make millions of dollars touring sold-out arenas. (We'll cover more about artists in Chapter 3: All About Artists.)

BACKUP SINGER

Background singers will either be hired on an as-needed basis (such as in the recording studio) or could be part of the permanent group that works with the artist and travels to live performances. Freelance singers especially will need to be versatile and flexible, as you may have to learn music quickly and completely, without much time to prepare. Pay varies greatly among backup singers, depending on the experience and the artist they are working with. Some may go on to become leading singers themselves, but this is obviously a very competitive field.

SONGWRITER

Someone has to write the songs before they can be recorded and released. A songwriter, or lyricist, comes up with the actual words and melody of the song, either to be used by himself or herself, or by another person. Songwriters can get almost any amount of money—from next to nothing all the way up to six or seven digits per song—depending on how successful the song turns out to be.

COMPOSERS AND ORCHESTRATORS

A songwriter comes up with the words and melody, and then a composer will take that to create accompaniment—the music that is heard behind the singer, whether it be chords or piano backing. Some songs may only have piano or guitar accompaniment, but most often there are many other instruments needed. When these are all put together into one piece of music, it is called a score. Movies and video games need this type of musical work, of course, but sometimes songs you hear on the radio also need more complex arranging. An orchestrator will take the basic accompaniment provided by the composer, and then figure out parts for drums, violins, synthesized electronic sounds, and more—whatever the song may need. Since the job market is very competitive, some in this field may only make $5,000 per year. However, some composers for huge movies may make up to $2 million for one movie's worth of work.

COPYIST

The songwriter and composer both have important jobs to do, but a copyist is responsible for physically turning their work into readable sheet music for every single voice or instrument that will be used when that song is performed. While orchestrators built up the score, a copyist will break it back down into its smaller pieces. This can mostly be done with computer programs like Sibelius and Finale. Copyists are usually paid by the page; more experienced copyists will earn a higher rate that those who are just beginning. Some successful copyists earn up to $80,000 per year.

A&R SCOUT

Major record labels have A&R (Artists and Repertoire) agents who travel all over the country (and world) looking for new artists and new material. Many of them are musicians of a similar age and genre to the artists they are trying to recruit. These agents spend all their time networking with musicians and other industry professionals. They attend live performances, listen to demos, talk to artists, and cultivate musicians who may not be ready to release a record. When an agent negotiates a contract with an artist, he or she is supported by a whole department of entertainment lawyers and has all the resources of the label at his or her command. A&R staff also participate in selecting songs for an album, and finding backup musicians to accompany the artist. Anywhere from $20,000 to $60,000 is what scouts typically make in a year.

ARTIST MANAGER

An artist manager works for the artist, finding jobs for the best possible pay. They might help negotiate contracts, book events for the artist, and give valuable advice to help steer the artist in the best direction. The pay for an artist manager varies depending on how much the artist himself or herself if making; generally, artist managers will get anywhere from 10 percent to 25 percent of what the artist earns. For this job, you need a fairly strong business background, along with knowledge of the music industry.

PRODUCER

A producer is one of the people near the top of the totem pole, so to speak. This person organizes the process of creating an album or song by helping to find talent, working on the contracts for all of the people involved, scheduling and supervising the recording, and overseeing the marketing team—all while trying to stay in budget and on time. Some artists have had success acting as their own producers. Most producers work for a fixed fee of the profits, making a total anywhere from pocket change up to tens of thousands of dollars for one project.

AUDIO ENGINEER

An audio engineer sets up and operates the recording equipment in the recording studio. They record, edit, and mix the sound to produce the final product. Most in this occupation earn from $25,000 per year to $150,000 per year.

BOARD OPERATOR/AUDIO ENGINEERS

In a concert, someone has to operate the soundboard and make sure the entire system is producing the right sound. Volume levels need to be perfect, and the right mix needs to be found so that everyone can enjoy the experience. These audio engineers can make from $60,000 to $120,000 every year.

BOOKING AGENT

When an artist or band goes on tour, a booking agent arranges the cities and venues that will be visited. Some artists are better suited for, or prefer, smaller and more personal sites for their performances, and some share their music in stadiums with huge, complex stages. Opening or supporting acts also need to be scheduled that fit well with the main artist. In the beginning, some booking agents may only make around $2,000 per year, but some may eventually make more than $1,000,000.

INTERN

Everyone has to start somewhere. Many of the people who now work in the music industry began as unpaid interns. Yes, there's a lot of grunt work involved—getting everyone else his or her coffee, running to the store last minute to buy batteries for recording equipment, and making copies— but a hard worker will impress the people who have experience, and a good reputation in the small things will lead to bigger opportunities sooner rather than later. Plus, you may get to meet some really cool people and get some valuable on-the-job training!

♫ FAST FACT

Pink Floyd — the famous British rock band — started out as a band of college students.

The following jobs would not generally be found attached to a record label, but they're also heavily involved in the music industry.

MUSIC EDITOR

When you watch a movie and the music in the background shows perfectly what's happening in the scene, you know you are seeing the work of a good music editor. Even if he or she didn't write the music, the editor knew how to find music that is the right tempo and style, and added in the music at the right time and at the right volume. Pay can vary from around $1,000 per week to $5,000 per week.

RADIO DISC JOCKEY (DJ)

A DJ on the radio will mix and play music, then chat about news, current events, music, and other interesting topics between the songs, as well as interview artists. There is a difference between a DJ and a radio personality—an on-air personality does not actually mix or play music. Those involved with radio will also schedule the lineup of music and commercials to be played. Different time slots will earn DJs different salaries; someone working the overnight shift will not make as much money as someone who is on the air while drivers are commuting to work and listening to the radio in their cars. The average radio DJ earns around $28,000 per year, but some can make up to $1,000,000 per year.

NIGHTCLUB DISC JOCKEY (DJ)

A Club DJ would play the music at a nightclub, bar, rave, or party using various types of music — vinyl records, CDs, or MP3s. A DJ spinning the tunes traditionally would need a mixer, two turntables, a sound system, and headphones; however, many now use digital mixing software. As a DJ in a club, you might get paid in drink tickets, or you might make millions of dollars a year. Sources say $300 per night is normal.

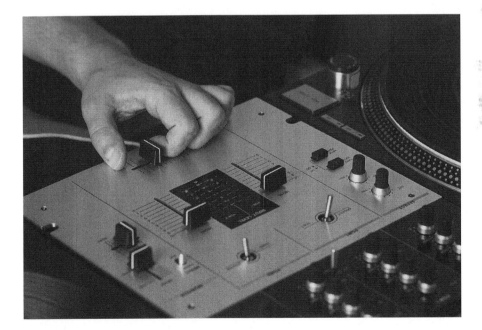

CONCERT PROMOTER

Live music can happen in a Midwestern arena, in a California bar, in a Texas honky-tonk, in a New York City theater, or following a rodeo concert. However, nobody will know about it if there isn't publicity. A promoter works with both the label and the venue where the artist will perform to make sure there is marketing and exposure to draw a big crowd. From understanding contract law to knowing graphic design, from marketing strategies to physically helping the band members set up their equipment, a promoter might be called on to do various jobs. Pay is almost always based per event, but the major players in this field can earn a million dollars or more per year with large events and popular stars.

MUSIC JOURNALIST

A music journalist writes for websites, newspapers, or magazines about artists and the music industry. They need to research and produce written work quickly, know the latest music news, and attend release parties and live concerts to get up-close-and-personal information. Of course, you will need to have solid writing skills. A background in music is helpful, so you know what you're talking about. You could make $15,000 to $30,000 a year (or more).

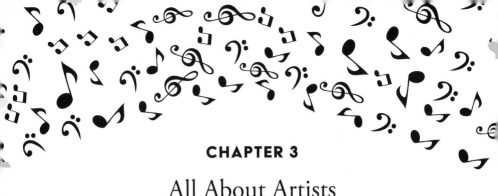

CHAPTER 3

All About Artists

A record label helps artists promote and sell their music. The two partners work together. The artists contribute their music and talent, and the record label contributes everything else: financing, production and recording expertise, manufacturing and shipping, distribution, and publicity. Both partners must work hard to make sure the music receives all the attention it deserves. When music stops receiving attention, it stops selling. It is important that the artists and the staff of the record label are deeply committed and hard working.

Record labels are very cautious when hiring artists, because they become part of the label's identity and image. Inexperience and lack of professionalism can add thousands of dollars to your production costs. A band that is unavailable for tours and public appearances makes promotion difficult. An artist may simply lack that special something that captures the heart and imagination of an audience.

And just as importantly, artists should not rush into a partnership with a music record before doing some research. If you are wanting to work with a record label, remember that when you are ready to sign your next new artist, he or she will look at your label's track record of past successes. A trail of mediocre CDs and a history of failure will not inspire other artists to sign with you in the future.

But first, there has to be music to release, and every song has to have someone perform it. Whether you want to be an artist yourself, recruit artists for
a record label, or just want to get familiar with issues relating to artists, here
are some things you need to know.

HOW ARE ARTISTS FOUND?

Thousands of artists are out there, waiting to be discovered and signed by
a record label. They are performing at clubs, raves, festivals, basement parties, talent quests, open mic nights (events where amateurs are allowed to
perform onstage for a few minutes each), and even on street corners. They
are posting their videos on YouTube and Facebook and submitting their
demos to every label that will accept them. A record label's job is to search
through the crowd of musicians trying to get their attention and find an
artist who has real talent, is a skilled musician, has great songs, is not signed
by another record label, and wants to work with them.

Identify with your genre

What kind of music do you like best? Country? R&B? Jazz? These (and others, of course) are examples of genre, meaning a certain type of something—
in this case, music.

Your passion for music will be the driving force behind the success of
your record label. By identifying yourself with a particular genre or style of
music, you will automatically attract the attention of the people who love
that music. In time, people will hear that kind of music and think of your
name.

Some genres—such as gospel, R&B, soul, country, jazz, heavy metal, and
hip-hop—are easily identifiable. Other genres are gradually emerging and

may not be as clearly defined. Traditional genres are constantly evolving, borrowing from other styles, or branching off into sub-genres. The music played on country radio stations today barely resembles the music of country music stars from three decades ago, while the music played on pop radio stations now incorporates many conventions of country music, such as the use of simple chord progressions, plaintive vocals, and the sounds of banjos and harmonicas. Genres such as modern zydeco, which evolved from Louisiana Creole dance music, and reggaeton or Latin urban music are rapidly changing mixtures of older genres. Identify yourself with one genre or sub-genre and focus on it until you have two or three successes under your belt. After you have established a solid reputation for your label, you can consider experimenting with a new direction. (Many artists and labels have done this successfully!)

♫ FAST FACT

In the late 1980s, MCA (now Universal Music) launched Mechanic Records to release heavy metal music and signed bands such as Voivod, Dream Theater, Bang Tango, and Trixter.

Dive into your chosen genre. Listen to the newest artists as well as the old favorites. Read reviews, blogs, zines, and magazines. Listen to internet radio, college radio stations, and commercial radio stations to see what songs are being played. Attend music festivals and go to clubs. Study the audiences; observe how they are dressed, how they behave, and how they react to the performers. Take note of what other record labels of the same genre are doing to promote their artists. Talk to fans. The more you become involved in your particular scene, the sharper your instincts will become, which will benefit you in any area of music industry.

TALES FROM THE INDUSTRY: Marvin Gaye

"Here, My Dear," an Album Ahead of Its Time

When Marvin Gaye's first wife, Anna Gordy, filed for divorce in 1975, he was in financial difficulties because of what he spent on expensive cars and vacation homes. Marvin's attorney came up with a unique way for him to pay Gordy the $600,000 he owed her in alimony and child support: a contract giving her half the royalties from his next project. In the spring of 1976, Gaye set out to give Motown a "lazy, bad" album, but as he worked on the music, his feelings about his troubled marriage and divorce were expressed in songs such as "I Met a Little Girl," "Anna's Song," "You Can Leave, But It's Going to Cost You," "Anger," and "Falling in Love." At first, Gaye was reluctant to release the album because it was so personal, but under pressure from Motown, it was released with the title "Here, My Dear," in December 1978.

Consumers hated the album, and critics called it "bizarre" and "un-commercial." An angry Gaye refused to promote it any further and went into self-imposed exile until 1982. In early 1979, only months after it came out, Motown also stopped promoting *Here, My Dear.* The album was Gaye's lowest-charting studio album of the 1970s, peaking at number four R&B and number 26 pop and falling off the charts after only two months. Its only single, "A Funky Space Reincarnation," peaked at number 23 on the R&B charts.

In 1994, the album was re-released in remembrance of the tenth anniversary of Gaye's untimely death. It reached number one on *Billboard*'s R&B catalog chart. Audiences in the 1990s identified with the raw emotions and intensely personal messages in the songs, and appreciated the Latin beats and Jazz fusion that had repelled listeners in the 1970s. Today "Here, My Dear" is considered a landmark in Gaye's career. *Mojo Magazine* (1995) named it as one of the greatest albums in music history. In 2003, it was ranked #462 in *Rolling Stone Magazine*'s critics' poll, "500 Greatest Albums of All Time."

It all starts locally

As with so many other things in life, word of mouth is important in the music industry—someone will recommend an artist to a label, or someone from the label will notice that a particular artist is attracting crowds at local venues.

TIP: Get to know people!

Build a network of eyes and ears — contacts who will remember you and let you know when they spot real talent. Become a regular at local clubs and music venues. Talk to sound engineers, DJs (disc jockeys), and bartenders about popular local musicians. You'll find out valuable information — about other artists or for yourself. Get to know the local bar owners. Ask to be put on the guest list for CD launch parties and other promotional events put on by clubs and radio stations. These are the same people who will help you in the future; it's helpful to build your network of resources now!

Read the music reviews in local newspapers and news magazines. Attend performances in music stores and open mic nights on college campuses and in coffee shops. Go to outdoor events where local bands are entertaining. When a tour or group visits your area, go talk to their entourage. See who is opening for a well-known act. All of the information you discover will help you find interesting potential artists, or learn some tricks and tools as an artist yourself.

SIGNS OF A GOOD ARTIST

Musical talent alone does not guarantee the success of a record. To succeed, an artist not only has to sound good, but also he or she has to appeal to his or her audience, be able to stick to a recording budget, and actively participate in the promotion of the record when it is released. What do record labels look for in an artist? The following qualities are important!

Has originality

Many people out there might be excellent musicians and can put on a great show, but they sound just like another well-known band or popular artist. The one who gets noticed is an artist who adds a new twist to the genre with unique vocal qualities, creative musical styling, and/or original lyrics. Music fans are always looking for something new.

Has appeal

Audiences unconsciously identify with the person singing the words and playing the music. Physical attractiveness helps, but even more important is the artist's personality that the audience sees and hears. The artist shows this self by his or her music, lyrics, behavior on stage, style of dress, and the images portrayed in music videos and publicity photos. Janis Joplin, one of the greatest female rock vocalists, didn't fit the stereotypes regarding physical beauty for female musicians, but her unique vocal quality, emotional intensity, and look captivated audiences across the world.

Is a good fit for the label (and vice versa!)

Do the artist and the label fit together? A brilliant artist who doesn't match the genre and style of the other recordings on a label might confuse its market. On the other hand, an artist won't want to work with a label that is trying to force him or her to be a certain way, or perform certain music if it's not his or her passion.

Has a market for his or her music

Consider who will buy the artist's songs. An artist may be talented and a good performer, but if his or her genre is not popular right now or is appreciated by only a tiny segment of the population, nobody can expect his or her CD to become a runaway bestseller or for everyone on Spotify to be listening to his or her music.

Has the right image

Every genre of music is associated with a lifestyle, as well as a certain type of dress and behavior. The artist's appearance on stage and visual image will help to market his or her music. Record labels will be looking for an artist to dress and act in a way that will appeal to its audience. An artist can be groomed to look and behave in a certain way, but an artist who already cultivates the right image will make the label's work much easier.

Has an established fan base

A new CD by an unknown artist attracts little attention among the thousands of other CDs in a music store. A pre-existing fan base gives music sales a jump-start. News of a release spreads like wildfire through social media—every fan wants to be the first to tell others about the new album and register an opinion.

Able to give consistent live performances

Some artists make beautiful recordings in the studio but aren't as fun to watch on the stage in front of a live audience. Live performances are important to a successful marketing strategy. A great artist should be able to create an intensely moving experience for live audiences, night after night and sometimes several times in one day. Not everyone has the ability to generate a commanding stage presence whenever and wherever it is required. Record labels observe artists to see how he or she handles awkward moments and interacts with listeners. They will talk to stage hands or the club manager about the artist. They will try to find out what bands the artist has performed with, and how long he or she has been performing in public.

Willing to travel and make public appearances

Let's be real—when you're trying to follow your dreams, you still have to pay the rent. Some artists may have another job or other responsibilities that make it difficult to travel.

Other artists may have opinions about not making public appearances at certain venues, such as parties, music stores, or festivals. As an artist, you need to be realistic and honest with yourself—and any potential label— about how much you can devote to your music career.

Has experience recording in a studio

Some bands can put on a heart-stopping performance onstage, but then have difficulty creating the same energy when they are in a studio without a live audience. Experienced artists already know how to recreate their sound in a studio environment and how to work with producers and sound engineers. Everyone involved in the production process knows money is being spent for every hour in the studio. A band or artist should help save everyone time and money by preparing in advance, cooperating with the sound engineer, and making the most of the time in the studio.

♫ FAST FACT

All four of the Beatles, Bob Dylan, Taylor Swift, and many other famous musicians cannot read music notation (**www.huffingtonpost .com**).

Is an accomplished musician

An artist with a trained voice and talent playing musical instruments has a great future in front of him or her. An amateur may be lucky enough to produce one or two really good songs, but he or she may not have the talent to expand this success to a whole album, let alone two or three. An accomplished musician can work easily with other musicians and pick up quickly on new ideas. It's not a horrible thing to be a beginner, but the artist must be dedicated to developing his or her talents, and the label must be willing to spend resources investing in the artist's progress.

Shows professional behavior

An artist should show up on time for appointments and respond to telephone calls and emails. It's simple professional courtesy to treat others with respect and cooperate well with other musicians, sound staff, and stage hands. Creative people sometimes have difficult personalities. If temperamental or unstable behavior is likely to interfere with production or jeopardize live performances, a label might (and should) think twice about signing. A "bad boy" or "bad girl" image is a plus in some genres, but the bad behavior should not extend to professional relationships.

Writes his or her own material

In some genres, it is common practice for a musician to perform songs written by independent songwriters. However, musicians of modern genres such as rap, reggae, punk, and emo often write their own lyrics and music. An artist or band that performs its own material or has its own songwriters is a plus. The label will be happy that it will not have to do extra work to find good songs or secure rights to music, and will be able to earn extra income from music publishing.

Has no contracts with any other record label

Labels are looking for an artist who has never had a contract with another label. If an artist is already signed with one label but wants to leave it, everyone involved will need to look into the old contract in detail before the next steps can be taken. Some artists assume they can walk away from an old contract, especially if the label is not working actively with them or if they have already completed a recording. Nobody wants to produce a record and then have the artist sued for breach of contract by another label.

Financially stable

It's difficult to work with an artist who is desperate for money. Many young artists don't understand that it takes time for a new record to start earning a profit and may have unrealistic expectations. Major records often offer artists an advance—a payment later recovered from sales of the record—

when they sign a contract. However, a young independent label might not have the cash reserves to give advances to artists. It is important that the artist clearly understands how he or she will be paid before the contract is signed to avoid any conflict over money.

Drugs and alcohol

How many newspaper articles have you read about a musician overdosing on drugs in a hotel room, or a band canceling a concert tour because one of its members has checked into a rehab center? Unfortunately, the music industry is known for its party culture. Music labels are cautious about hiring someone with known substance abuse problems. Even if an artist can manage drug or alcohol use so it does not interfere with recording sessions, sooner or later it will get out of hand. Drug and alcohol abuse often intensifies when an artist is on the road and can lead to erratic and uncontrolled behavior onstage and in public.

Underage artists

There are laws in each state that talk about contracts for artists under the age of 18. Minors are typically allowed to break a contract after they have signed because of their age and inexperience. Parents or guardians usually have to sign the contract and be present at performances and recording sessions. In many states, before anyone signs a contract, a court hearing must determine whether it is in the best interests of the minor. Don't listen to these words as discouragement! There are young performers out there, of course. If music truly is in your heart, don't let your age stop you from succeeding!

WHAT DOES AN ARTIST LOOK FOR IN A RECORD LABEL?

When an artist is considering signing with a label, it can't be a quick decision. The artist is trusting the company with his or her career. The label could make the artist famous . . . or stall his or her career before it even begins.

♫ FAST FACT

During the first decade of the 21st century, like all major record labels, Warner Music Group evolved to adapt to rapid changes in the way music is distributed through digital media. It moved out of record production and sold off its manufacturing operations in 2003. At the end of 2007, Warner became the third major label to sell digital music without Digital Rights Management (DRM), the technology that inhibits the use of digital media, through Amazon MP3 (Amazon. com's digital music store).

Here are some questions an artist will want to ask a record label before signing a contract:

- What other artists have signed with your label?

- How many successful CDs have you launched, and how successful were they?

- Have you had any notable failures?

- How do you get the music to the public? How do your distributors pay you? Do you do any advertising with them?

- What will you do to promote my record and me?

- What is your advertising budget for new releases?

- How much will I get paid from the sale of each record?

- What kinds of internet promotion do you use, and how do you handle internet sales?

- Do you have relationships with independent radio stations or promoters?

- How many other artists are you working with now?

- Who will pay for travel expenses when I go on tour?

- Who will select the producer and the recording studio?

- Are you offering an advance? (Sometimes artists get paid a certain amount before the actual sales start coming in, but sometimes you only get paid for each piece of music that is actually sold.)

- What do you expect from me?

UNDERSTANDING EACH OTHER

Many artists, especially if they are young, don't understand all of the legal words in a contract, even when they have a lawyer to review it for them. They may assume that the money will come pouring in as soon as their CDs are released, or they might not understand that they are expected to pay part of the costs to produce the music. To avoid an awkward situation later, artists and labels need to sit down and talk about what each section of the contract means in real terms. The artist should know about royalties, copyrights, and publishing laws—and when they'll get paid.

The artist may need to know about how the music is going to be produced and distributed, and the costs involved so he or she is on board. Also, artists need to know a bit about marketing and promotion, and what they should do to advertise themselves. The most successful CDs are made by artists who aggressively promote themselves by appearing in the media and in public, blogging and communicating with their fans through Twitter and email, performing live whenever they can, and trying to establish ongoing relationships with their audiences. An artist who understands that will make a greater effort.

The most important thing is communication. Everyone involved should not be afraid to ask questions to make sure he or she is understanding. Find out what's important to your label and discover what the artist hopes your collaboration will accomplish. When everyone understands how both sides think and feel, you can better plan how to appeal to your target audience as a team and market your music.

CHAPTER 4

Contracts and Agreements

A record label needs legal contracts and agreements to function. Contracts give it the right to record, copy, and sell music, art, and film media. Written agreements and contracts are important tools of the trade. A contract explains how everyone will make money. It also attempts to think of every circumstance that could possibly affect the business and to protect everyone involved from financial loss.

Don't panic—you're going to see words that might be unfamiliar to you. It may seem weird, and you may be tempted to ignore some parts of a contract, but it is absolutely necessary for you (and your parents or guardians, if you are under the age of 18) to be familiar and comfortable with the legal parts of your business. Young artists sometimes mistakenly sign away important rights. A mistake in a contract could cost you an opportunity to earn millions or send the whole company into bankruptcy. Take time to learn the legal language and study your contracts carefully. Find a lawyer who can explain each part until you understand it. For extra credit, go check out contracts other record labels or artists use. You might be able to find examples through on online search, your lawyer, or other contacts in the music industry.

GET EVERYTHING IN WRITING

In your grandparents' day, people sealed their partnerships with a hand-shake. That doesn't go far in today's world—at least when it comes to protecting either side from trouble down the line. Never rely on a verbal agreement or a handshake to seal a deal. Agreements that seem perfectly clear during a discussion over lunch or in a club after a performance suddenly become fuzzy when money is involved. Young professionals in particular may be carried away by the excitement of the moment and make promises that are later forgotten. Always carry a notebook and write down the details of any commitments the other party makes. Ask for specifics such as delivery dates and deadlines. Type up the information as soon as possible, and have the other party sign the document acknowledging that they accept the arrangement. At the very least, get an email confirming the other party has read your notes and agrees with the terms. In many states, an email is not legally binding, but it is written evidence that on a specific date the other party acknowledged making certain commitments.

In a 2013 *Forbes* article, Oliver Herzfeld summarizes a New York state lawsuit where a car owned by Gelco Corporation, which provides fleet management services and consumer car and truck financing, caused damage to a car driven by John Forcelli. While the case was in court, a Gelco representative offered Forcelli $230,000 to settle the case during a phone conversation and followed up the phone conversation with an email to his attorney stating that "per our phone conversation today, May 3, 2011, you accepted my offer of $230,000 to settle this case."

When the New York Supreme Court dismissed Forcelli's claim a week later, Gelco tried to get out of paying him $230,000. When Gelco appealed, the New York Appellate Division agreed with the ruling of the lower court, and Gelco had to pay Forcelli $230,000.

To avoid situations like that, Herzfeld advises, "Offers, counter-offers and terms of proposed agreements communicated via email should explicitly state that they are subject to any relevant conditions, as well as to the further review and comment of the sender's clients and/or colleagues."

He then offers a few disclaimers that all emails related to figuring out the details of contracts should contain. The email should be clear to state that it:

- "is not an offer capable of acceptance"

- "does not evidence an intention to enter into an agreement"

- "has no operative effect until a definitive agreement is signed in writing by both parties"

Everyone involved, according to Herzfeld, should know that "no party should act in reliance on the email or any representations of the sender until a definitive agreement is signed in writing by both parties."

While this isn't a music industry-specific example, it is an easy-to-understand case demonstrating that caution is necessary when negotiating contracts in an internet-dominated world.

Don't think of email communication as informal, and always keep good records!

♫ FAST FACT

119 million people listen to online radio for an average of 12 hours and 53 minutes per week (**www.digitaltrends.com**).

FINDING A LAWYER

Sooner or later, anybody in the music industry will need the help of a good lawyer to understand or enforce a contract. Don't wait around until you're in trouble to find a lawyer.

Most bigger-than-average record companies have their own legal teams that take care of contracts. If you are working for a label like this, make sure you get to know people in the legal department. If you are an artist, or if you are working independently, you might need to find your own lawyer.

The best way to find a good entertainment lawyer is to ask other record labels and artists who they recommend. You could also search local business directories and law directories such as Lawyers.com (**www.lawyers .com**). Make an appointment to interview the lawyer by phone or in person. Some lawyers offer a free first consultation. Prepare a list of questions in advance, and ask the lawyer about his or her experiences, especially in the music industry. Ask for references or the names of other clients. If the lawyer makes a good impression but does not seem knowledgeable about your field or you do not feel satisfied with his or her answers, look for someone else.

WHAT TO ASK A PROSPECTIVE ENTERTAINMENT LAWYER

- What is your experience in the music industry?

- Do you have references or other clients I can contact?

- Here are my financial records. Do you see anything that I need to be concerned about or need extra protection for?

- What use of my music by another artist would constitute copyright infringement?

Find an affordable lawyer who has a personality you like, and who communicates easily. This person may be negotiating with others on your behalf; you need to feel confident he or she can represent you well. A lawyer should be personally involved in your projects and believe you have the potential to succeed; this kind of person may be willing to offer free advice sometimes or negotiate lower fees. Really great and experienced entertainment lawyers are usually located in large cities and can be expensive, but if you find yourself in a complicated contract tug-of-war, the extra expense is worth it.

WHEN AN ARTIST SIGNS A CONTRACT

Awesome news! You're an artist that has been offered a contract with a record label! What now? Do you jump in with both feet? Hold on there!

Some artists may be so eager to sign with a record label that they give up their right to their own lawyer or so naive that they trust the record label's lawyer to draft a fair contract. Even though the contract may seem fair, artists should have their contracts reviewed by a separate lawyer for their own protection. Many organizations, such as Volunteer Lawyers for the Arts (**www.vlany.org**), which provides services for artists located in New York, and California Lawyers for the Arts (**www.calawyersforthearts.org**), provide free or low-cost legal advice for artists.

In a contract negotiation, the lawyer representing the artist will try to increase the amount the artist receives in royalties, secure at least partial ownership of publishing rights and the master recording, and ensure the artist is not signing away valuable rights. It's for the artist's own benefit to invest in a lawyer before signing a contract.

ARTIST'S AGREEMENT

An artist's agreement can be the simple two-page contract independent labels usually use or a 50-page document like the one major record labels use, which outlines complex arrangements and explains what will be done in every kind of situation that may come up. It explains what the artist will do for the record label, what the record label will do for the artist, and what will happen if either party fails to do their parts. Artist's agreements vary widely in content and form, but all of them contain the same basic pieces:

- Term of the contract

- Territory

- Services

- Recording commitment

- Recording procedure

- Recoupable costs

- Advances

- Rights granted to the recording company

- Royalties

- Definitions

- Accounting

- Publishing

- Warranties

- Indemnity

- Suspension or termination

- Group provisions

- Merchandising rights

- Music videos

- Websites and digital rights

- Additional provisions

Term of the contract

The term is how long the contract will be going. A period of time might be given, but record label contracts typically define the term by the number of songs or albums the artist will record for the label under the contract. Why? Lots of things could delay the release of an album. A band might be too busy touring to create and record new material, or recording might be paused by personal and family problems. There may be technical issues or legal delays. You also don't want to have too much of a good thing; taking time between releasing albums is a good thing, because it keeps people wanting more.

The term usually talks about an initial period (also known as initial term or first contract period) followed by several one-sided options for the record label to extend the contract for an additional period. Each option means another recording.

The initial period begins on the date the contract is signed and can extend for a period of several months after the first album's street date (the day the album is officially released) or delivery date (the date the master recording is completed and delivered to the record label). At that point, the record label can use its option to extend the contract or the contract renews automatically (unless the record label indicates it wants to terminate the contract).

Pay attention to renewal dates

Everyone should keep track of renewal dates and note whether the contract renews automatically or if it renews only if the label wants it to. If a contract renews automatically, the label could be forced to record another unsuccessful album for an artist whose first album didn't sell. If the contract doesn't renew automatically and the label doesn't tell the artist before the given date, there goes the chance to release another winning album.

TERRITORY

Territory means where the contract counts. The territory for a music contract is typically "the world" or "the universe" because music created in one country is often sold in another.

SERVICES

Services is talking about what an artist is promising to the record label. A record label contract usually claims an artist's exclusive services, which means the artist will be breaking the contract if he or she records for any other company. The contract may make exceptions for certain types of recorded events, such as a large music festival, and nonmusical performances, including movie roles or television interviews, might not count. Many contracts will allow an artist to act as a producer for another musician. A record label can agree to a side artist agreement, which lets the artist perform as a backup singer in another artist's recording.

RECORDING COMMITMENT

The recording commitment tells you exactly how much material the artist is expected to record. Most say one full album of new material in every contract period, with an album being a certain number of minutes. The contract might allow other things for special occasions, like a single original song for a charity fundraiser. Usually this means not recording more than the length of one full album. The contract usually doesn't include things like Christmas albums or a set of previously released songs.

RECORDING PROCEDURE

Remember the questions you learned in writing class—Who, What, Where, Why, and How? This section of the contract kind of answers those questions. When, where, and how will the music be recorded? It can be as simple as a time and place, or it can outline detailed steps to take, such as creating budgets, choosing producers, and turning in expense reports. It also talks about tax forms and how the producer is chosen and paid.

♫ FAST FACT

Perfect pitch — the ability to replicate a note perfectly without a reference note — is a rare auditory phenomenon that famous musicians like Mozart allegedly had.

The recording procedure should give the record label the job of approving a recording budget. The artist gives a recording budget to the record label several weeks before recording. If the label thinks the budget is too high, the artist must make some changes. If things get too expensive because of delays in the studio or extra costs, the artist has to pay out of his or her own pocket. Once a budget is approved, the money is put into a special account used to pay bills and make purchases.

THE IMPORTANCE OF A RECORDING BUDGET

The cost of making a record is huge. After the recording is done, it will take several weeks before the CD is released and money starts to trickle in from sales. Payments from sellers may not arrive in the label's bank account until two or three months after that. A recording budget helps keep the money under control and makes sure there is enough cash on hand to market the CD when it is drops.

RECOUPABLE COSTS

Some costs in making a CD are recoupable, meaning the record label pays these expenses first and then is paid back by the artist through royalties.

Expenses that are always recoupable are:

- Recording costs: Studio rentals, producers, mixers, sound engineers, backup musicians and vocalists, technical staff, and travel expenses

- Advances: Money paid directly to the artist before sales

- Tour support: Money paid to the artist to help with the cost of going on tour: food and hotels, equipment, bus or van rentals, and travel

Expenses that are sometimes recoupable:

- Music videos: The cost of making a music video is typically recoupable from royalties from the video and sometimes also the royalties from the album.

- Promotional costs: Some labels will take back all or part of the cost of any marketing or promotion done specifically for the artist and the artist's albums.

Expenses that are not recoupable:

- Cost of making and packaging CDs and vinyls

- Distribution costs: Shipping, money paid to distributors, promotional items

- Graphics and photography

Non-recoupable expenses are usually taken from the money received from CD sales before royalties are added up, so the record label is still reimbursed. The difference is that the reimbursement does not come out of the artist's royalties.

As you can see, it could be a long time before the artist collects any money. Some artists never collect any royalties because these costs are never paid off. This can happen when the record label spends a lot to promote an album, when recording costs are high, or when sales volume is low.

Don't worry, though—album royalties aren't the only way an artist makes money. An artist who writes his or her own songs will also get a mechanical royalty for each song on the album. Mechanical royalties are collected on the use of copyrighted, published material. The artist can also earn money from live performances and concerts, merchandise sales, and performance royalties. Performance royalties are earned when a song is played on the radio and are collected and distributed by The American Society of Composers, Authors, and Publishers (ASCAP) and Broadcast Music Inc. (BMI).

ADVANCES

An advance is money given to an artist before the recording has started. Advances are recoupable from the artist's royalties.

Large record labels sometimes handle this by setting up a recording fund that is a lot more than the recording budget. The artist gets to keep whatever is left after the recording costs are paid off. The advance helps pay an artist's personal expenses while he or she is touring or composing and recording full time. Small independent labels usually cannot achieve the same level of sales as large labels and will never recoup their recording costs, let alone a large advance, from the artist's royalties.

RIGHTS GRANTED TO THE RECORDING COMPANY

What rights does the record label have to the artist's work? The record label usually owns the master recordings and the right to use the artist's name and likeness to promote the albums.

Even when the rights to a recording have been assigned to a record label, copyright law allows an artist to legally reclaim the copyright after 35 years (if it was written after 1978) unless the recording is a "work for hire." Reclaiming can be tricky to do for a recording itself, because the term "for hire" can mean different things to the artist, the songwriter, the label, or the publisher.

However, it's not as hard for the songwriter to reclaim rights. (Paul McCartney of the Beatles has made headlines recently in his battle to gain the copyrights from the Beatles songs he wrote, currently owned by Sony. Unfortunately for Sir Paul, the law states that songs written before 1978 need 56 years before the original copyright can be terminated.) Some smaller record labels might allow the artists to use the material for promotion on their own, if the budget for marketing isn't that large.

Saying you own the copyright to the master recording is not the same as owning the copyright to the song itself. If a label wants to receive money when the artist's song is performed on *Glee* or *The Voice*, this should be addressed in a separate section on Publishing Rights.

 **FAST FACT**

Spotify, the music streaming service, began as a small Swedish startup in 2006.

ROYALTIES

Royalties are how much the artist makes from each album or song. Before the royalty is paid out, some things are taken from the total, like the following:

- Packaging (container charge): printing labels, inserts, and covers for vinyls and packaging CD cases or covers, usually around 25 percent of the list price of the CD

- Distribution costs: packing and shipping, and the amount paid to a distribution company, usually $2 to $3 per CD

- Reserves: A certain number of CDs will be returned for refunds after retailers are unable to sell them.

- Free goods: The record label will not pay royalties on free CDs handed out for publicity purposes to radio stations and retail outlets or given away in promotions. (This accounts for around 15 percent of the list price.)

In the U.S., artists will typically make 10 to 20 percent from every album sold on royalties, but the amount would be lower from sales in other countries. If more than one artist is in the group, the royalties are shared.

Example of a royalty calculation

Retail Price of CD		$15.00
Distribution		-$2.00
Packaging	25%	-$3.75
Free goods	15%	-$2.25
Reserves for returns	15%	-$2.25
Royalty Base Price		$4.75
Artist's royalties	15%	$0.71
Producer's royalties	2%	$0.10
Net Artist Royalties		$0.62

Royalties for music videos

Artists and labels usually split the royalties that are made from music videos 50/50. If a different agreement is going to be used, the contract will spell it out.

Royalties for internet downloads

Times they are a-changing. In the music industry, new technology is quickly changing how music is sold. From vinyl records to cassette tapes and 8-track tapes, then to CDs and MP3 players, there have been many forms of getting music to the people. Now any number of devices can download and play digital music.

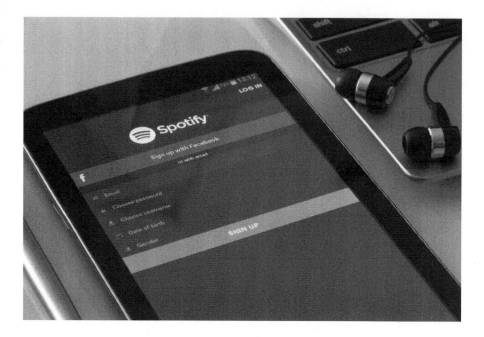

Even when there is no packaging cost for a digital download, some labels continue to deduct 25 percent from the sales price for packaging. This is because the cost of changing to the different technologies still costs the label. They may split the sales of digital downloads equally between the artist and the label.

When are royalties paid?

The artist doesn't get paid royalties until the record label makes money on the sales of the music. This could be several months after the records are ordered and shipped, so the amount paid as royalties might not look the same as the sales figures reported by the record label. And, of course, the artist won't get any royalties until all advances have been recovered.

Royalties for producers and mixers

Sometimes a producer is a paid employee of a record label. Sometimes they are per-job freelancers. If that is the case, the artist pays the producer a percentage of his or her royalties. Even though the artist is the one actually responsible for this, most record labels do the math and send out the paychecks for the artist. The producer typically doesn't get paid until the main costs of recording have been repaid from the artist's royalties. After that, the producer continues to receive his or her part of the royalties.

Changing the way royalties are calculated

A record label might say that it has the right to change the way it pays out royalties if its sales strategy changes. A new form of digital technology might arise, or the label might discover that the artists' fans like vinyl albums. The record label might give away fewer free CDs or downloads than it had first budgeted for. The contract should explain how these changes are made so the artist keeps getting paid about the same percentage.

Changes to laws about royalties

Congress passed a life-changing law for songwriters in the summer of 2016. In essence, this law dictates that when two songwriters collaborate who are registered to two different PROs (Performance Rights Organizations are entities that collect royalties for songwriters), each PRO has the right to license out 100 percent of the song, without the consent of the other PRO, and without giving them any royalties. Let's say Artist A writes a song with Artist B. Artist A is registered to BMI (Broadcast Music Inc.), and Artist B is registered to ASCAP (American Society of Composers, Authors, and Publishers).

A moviemaker comes to ASCAP and says, "Hey, I want to put Artist B's song in my movie and give him millions of dollars." Artist A realizes this and says, "Hey, wait, I wrote that song, too, and I want millions of dollars, too!" ASCAP can respond, "Nah, because you're registered with BMI, not ASCAP," and the movie maker can respond, "Yeah, and I don't have to give any royalties to BMI, because I already paid them to ASCAP."

Many artists are concerned that this law discourages creativity and collaboration, and it lets a lot of musicians figuratively stab each other in the back for no reason.

TALES FROM THE INDUSTRY: Reprise Records

Frank Sinatra's Label Gave Up Its Rights to Its Artists' Work

The famous Frank Sinatra didn't have it bad working with Capitol/ EMI. But when Capitol/EMI wouldn't give him the artistic freedom he wanted, he decided to follow his heart and launch his own label in 1960. The result was Reprise Records.

The new chairman of the board, Sinatra appealed to many of his colleagues and friends and wound up signing on big names such as Dean Martin, Sammy Davis Jr., Bing Crosby, Jo Stafford, Rosemary Clooney, Esquivel, and stand-up comedian Redd Foxx. Each artist had full creative freedom and, eventually, complete ownership of his or her work, including publishing rights.

In 1963, Sinatra sold the label to Warner Bros. because of poor sales. Many of the original artists were dropped, and Warner-Reprise began to target teen audiences with a roster of emerging pop artists. Warner Bros. deactivated the label in 1976 but brought it back in 1987. Reprise still issues recordings Sinatra made while on the label and also put out collections of his greatest hits after his death in 1988.

Although this might have sounded awesome for artists, it meant that the label did not have a catalog of its early artists (Dean Martin, Jimi Hendrix, and The Kinks). Their records are being sold today through other labels. Dean Martin's recordings were out of print for nearly 20 years until Capitol Records began distributing them.

Definitions

The words used when talking about royalties can be hard to understand, and the way they're defined helps show how much money the artist will eventually be paid. Many contracts have a separate space for definitions, often written near the end of the contract.

Keep an eye out for these terms:

Container Charge: An artist is paid royalties on his or her music — not the plastic container of a CD, the paper and cardboard sleeves of a vinyl record, or the artwork on the cover. At least 25 percent is usually taken off from the sale price of an album to pay for its packaging.

Royalty Base Price: When you take off taxes, distribution costs, container charges, and other costs from the retail price of a record, this is what you get.

♫ FAST FACT

Universal Music Enterprises and Geffen now manage MCA's rock, pop, and urban back catalogs (including those from ABC Records and Famous Music Group). MCA's jazz, classical music, and musical theater are managed by other UMG subsidiaries.

UNDERSTAND THE DEFINITIONS!

Don't get taken for a ride! It can be hard to understand what a certain word means when the definitions are at the end of the contract. Get a lawyer to explain the terms of the contract in detail. When in doubt, ask questions. If the first album is a success, everyone will be inspired, excited, and willing to cooperate for the second one.

Accounting

How will the money part of the deal be handled, what kinds of financial statements will the artist will receive, and how can someone review or question these statements? This is where the accounting section comes in. This part of the contract tells how royalty earnings will be applied to advances and promotional costs.

Most record labels send out financial statements every six months. It is not necessary to send out a statement if no records have sold and no royalties have been earned, but showing a brief update keeps everyone up to speed. If royalties have been earned but the artist isn't being paid from them yet because of recoupable costs, the statement should show how they have been used to repay advances and other outstanding amounts.

Sales in foreign countries

This part of the contract will also talk about how sales outside the U.S. will be calculated and reported, what exchange rates will be used, and how often the money will be credited to the artist. Record labels may be working with companies based in those foreign countries, so delays in payments may happen because of currency changing.

Procedure for contesting the validity of a statement

What if the artist thinks there has been a mistake in his or her payments? This section tells how the accounting can be checked out, and how to contest it, if needed. For example, it could say that the artist has two years to notify the company that he or she wishes to contest a statement, and an audit will be performed within six months after the notice. If that audit uncovers anything shady, the artist has one year to take action. If the artist has not gone to court or settled the problem within a year, he or she is giving up the right to do so. The contract can also say who will do the audit—a lawyer not involved with either the record label or the artist. A lawsuit means legal costs. A good contract lays down the rules in case the relationship between the artist and the record company goes sour later on.

PUBLISHING

If you write a song, you have another way of bringing in money for you and for the record label—publishing rights. Congrats—you're a performer *and* a songwriter. Musicians get royalties whenever a song they recorded is sold as a single or as part of an album. Songwriters also earn mechanical royalties when one of their songs is sold as part of a recording; sold as a ringtone; played over the radio or in a movie or TV commercial; played in a dentist's office, an elevator, or the telephone while someone is on hold; included in a video game; sold as printed sheet music; or performed or recorded by another band (called a cover).

A songwriter assigns the copyright for a song to the music publisher, who acts as the songwriter's agent to license the song for the artist. The publisher and the songwriter usually share any profits equally—50/50—unless it says differently in the contract.

Publishing rights are significant moneymakers for artists. Recoupable costs are not taken from mechanical royalties because they are for what happens during the recording process, not during songwriting. A singer/songwriter may not get artist royalties from an album, but he or she will be paid mechanical royalties from sales of the album, plus any other use of the songs.

You will find more information about publishing music in Chapter 6.

MECHANICAL ROYALTIES

The first time a song is released, the mechanical royalties are negotiated between the record label and the songwriter or music publisher. Record labels usually get 75 percent for first-time releases of songs written and owned by the artist. Then, a reduced rate is given to other record labels to encourage them to use their artist's songs. Of course, the more famous the songwriter, the higher they will get paid for a new original song, but any re-recording will have a smaller rate. Royalty rates are adjusted for inflation; the contract will talk about this as well.

Cross-collateralization

Sometimes an artist may agree to apply some of his or her mechanical royalties to recording expenses. This might happen if the artist really wants to release an album but the record label worries it will not make its money back after recording costs. If expenses are paid back from income other than artist's royalties, such as mechanical royalties or the artist's royalties from future albums, this is called cross-collateralization. Cross-collateralization is risky to the artist—you're saying you'll give up your income from other sources to cover the cost of recording and promoting an album.

♬ FAST FACT

The expense of MCA's 1979 acquisitions combined with rising costs for the production of vinyl caused financial losses from 1979 until 1982, and the company did not begin to gain ground until the mid-1980s.

WARRANTIES

In a warranty, the artist makes a promise to the label that nothing will happen that could sabotage the recording. If any of these are later found to be untrue, the label can break the contract or sue for losses. You might see things in warranties like:

- The artist is old enough to legally sign a contract.

- The artist hasn't signed any other contract that would mess up this contract.

- The record label won't have to give out any more money than what is listed in the contract, or to anyone else but the artist.

- If there's a labor union around, the artist is a member in good standing.

- The artist owns the rights to all of the music he or she is putting on the recording or has a license to record the music.

- The artist hasn't recorded anything the record label doesn't know about.

The artist might also promise:

- To be available for interviews and live performances.

- Not to do anything that would keep him or her from seeing the contract through.

- Not to record for any other company or allow any live performances to be recorded without a signed, written agreement that the recording won't be used on a record.

- Not to re-record any of the songs on the record for a certain period of time.

- To let the record label know someone else is making or selling pirated copies of the record.

INDEMNITY

An indemnity clause means the artist has to pay if the record label is sued because of the artist's work. People do sue for copyright infringement after an artist has written and recorded a song. When the artist gets sued, so does the record label. Even if the lawsuit is thrown out or the artist wins, it can still cost everyone tens of thousands of dollars. In that case, the label will take those costs out of an artist's royalties.

SUSPENSION OR TERMINATION

What if things start to go wrong? What are the reasons someone might get fired? If that does happen, what happens next? Is money owed, and who owes what? This all is laid out in the contract. A suspension means there is a problem, and it needs to be fixed by a certain time. A termination means the whole deal is off—but this usually takes several months to complete.

It might go like this:

- Nine months after the contract is signed, if the record label hasn't recorded an album with the artist, the artist has 30 days to send the record label a written notice that he or she still wants to do the recording. If notice is not sent within 30 days, the artist loses the right to take any action.

- The record label has 60 days after this to send the artist a written notice regarding when recording an album might start.

- If the company hasn't sent this by the end of that 60-day period, the artist has 30 days to terminate the contract.

- Once the company gets the termination notice, the contract ends, except if there are any warranties or royalties still to be taken care of.

Force majeure

What if something huge comes up—like a natural disaster or accident? That's where this phrase comes in. "Force majeure" means "superior force." Every contract should include a force majeure clause that protects the label in case something happens that is beyond its control.

GROUP PROVISIONS

When you use the word "artist," that can mean more than one person. It can mean an ensemble or a band. In which case, the artist's agreement goes for all members of the group. If one person breaks the contract, it's as if the whole group broke the contract.

Many things are mentioned in this section. The band members will need to make sure that the name they choose isn't taken by another group. The contract will also have details about how to keep the record deal from being ruined if a band member suddenly decides to leave the group. The record label probably has final approval of any musician who replaces the band member who is leaving, to help make sure the band continues to be a success. The contract will note that, if a member does leave, the band name stays the same. However, if the entire band breaks up, nobody can use the name.

Sometimes artists leave a band to record a solo album. (Hello, Justin Timberlake? Beyoncé? Zayn Malik?) A leaving member option lets the record label sign him or her to a solo record deal under a contract that will be similar to the one signed by the group as a whole.

MERCHANDISING RIGHTS

An independent record label has the rights to sell the artist's picture and bio for use on things like hats, T-shirts, concert programs, and posters. In return, the artist gets part of the royalties that come from merchandise licensing. An independent record label might front the money so the artist can make and sell merchandise, or the label might produce the items itself and sell them to the artist, who then sells them at live performances.

MUSIC VIDEOS

When a new album drops, usually there's a music video (or two) right behind it. The record label has the right to release a music video but doesn't have to. When an artist makes a music video, it belongs to the label. The contract will say how the artist can help come up with ideas for the video, where and when it will be filmed, and who will be the producer. The budget is made before shooting. If the artist causes extra costs to come up, he or she has to pay for them, but not if the company's actions caused the budget to be blown. The contract also lists the royalties the artist will get from the music video.

WEBSITES AND DIGITAL RIGHTS

A band's website is important because it is the artists' public face to the world; lists concert schedules; sells CDs, digital downloads, and merchandise; and acts as a focal point for social media. It is one of the first places where fans from all over the world will look for information. A record label will want to be running the official website for several reasons. The website must be showcase the brand of the artist, look professional, and be kept up to date; an artist might not have the time to do this while touring. If news needs to be shared, the label needs to be able to post it right away. There is also the threat of hackers and scary cyber attacks. (It does happen!)

An artist's agreement usually lets the label run the artist's official website. The artist can have his or her own website as long as he or she clearly shows it is not the official site. The contract will talk about the royalties the artist will get from sales that come through the website. Because the record label owns the master recording, the contract should state if the artist can play recordings or show clips of live performances on his or her site.

♫ FAST FACT

The company that would become Sony Music Holdings had doubled its market share by 1970.

The contract should also tell who will be responsible for Facebook, Instagram, or Twitter pages and the artist's presence on music promotion sites such as PureVolume (**www.purevolume.com**). The contract may also specify where the fans can go to buy the artist's recordings digitally and how that will work. This is important because it's easier for people to pirate music illegally on certain sites, and some others have better reputations.

ADDITIONAL PROVISIONS

An artist's agreement typically includes additional provisions common to many types of legal contracts:

- Assignment—If anybody buys the company, he or she will have the rights to the contract.

- Notices—How will written notices be sent out and when the notice is considered to have been given (the date it is sent by registered mail).

- Confidentiality—Nobody can show the contract to anyone else without prior written permission.

- Jurisdiction—Which state laws are enforcing the contract.

- Entire agreement—No other written agreements that relate to the contract exist.

- Collective bargaining—Any details about unions go here.

- Severability—Even if one part of the contract is void because of a federal, state, or local law, the rest of the contract is legal. (Now you have a new word to add to your vocabulary!)

The contracts you will use in your career depend on the size of your record label. More details about contracts will be mentioned in later chapters.

CHAPTER 5

Recording and Producing

A label wants to make good music and sell it. An artist wants to share his or her creativity and talent with the world. Both need to work together to make the best music possible. If the actual recording is bad, a good band and a great song may never get noticed. A song that's just OK, on the other hand, can become a hit if it's well recorded. If you have a quality first album, your reputation will speak for itself. It's so important to learn as much as you can before you make your first record. If you don't feel like you have a lot of experience, find people who do—and learn all you can from them. Everything you learn from making your first record will help you to make your next one even better.

So, how does a record get produced? Well, it goes something like this:

- The artist finds enough songs for an album and practices them until they are perfect.

- The record label takes care of the details for recording: finding the studio, hiring the different people who will work on the album, getting equipment, and even making sure people have places to stay overnight and food catering for those long days. The artist might need to handle some of these things if those details are in the contract.

- The artist, sound engineer, and producer record the songs in the studio. Each song is "mixed" by an engineer who puts the tracks together. Everyone listens and gives feedback.

- The album is "mastered" to create the final recording: the songs are tweaked to make up for any weird sounds in the studio, blank space is put in between the songs, and songs recorded in different places are balanced so the whole album plays at the same volume.

- In the meantime, a label for the CD cover or vinyl album cover is designed and printed.

- The master recording, CD labels, and packaging are delivered to the manufacturer, who copies the album to CDs and packages them. The music is also sent out to those who sell it digitally online, along with graphics to be used on web pages.

- The packaged CDs are sent out to stores. At the same time, the record label begins the publicity for the new release.

That's the simple version — the actual recording process has more details, of course. It may look different depending on the genre of music and the skills of the artist and staff. Some studios and manufacturers have turnkey or all-in-one packages that put together several services and then give you a finished product. An artist or producer may have multiple skills and be involved in several aspects of the recording process. At each step, you will be faced with choices and decisions. But your goal should be to always produce the best quality you can, while making sure you have enough money to market and promote the record when it launches.

YOUR PRODUCTION BUDGET

Everybody needs to pay attention to the money side of the recording. A clear production budget will show you where you stand and help you make tough decisions. A budget also helps you plan ahead; when you see you are over budget, you will be able to make changes and still achieve your goals.

Make a list of how much everything will cost, from recording to publicity. Then add another 30 percent on top of that for the unexpected. If you don't have this much money available, you need to find other sources of cash, cut some things out of your project, or find cheaper ways to do what you want. Don't go forward just hoping everything will work out; make a plan.

PRODUCTION BUDGET FOR ALBUM

Every budget will be different, but here are things that go into planning your budget.

Recording	
Rehearsal space rental	Mastering
Studio fee X number of days	Tape copies, reference CDs
Drum Amp, Mic and Phase	Instruments
Recording tape	Shipping
Equipment rental	Fee for sound engineer
Transportation	Fees for side artists, backup
Lodgings while in studio	vocalists
Catering	Fee for producer
Mixing	

Music Video (to be paid back from Artist Royalties)	
Camera rental	Catering
Crew	Stage and construction
Processing and transfers	Transportation
Offline editing	Director's fee
Online editing	Support staff

Manufacturing	
Album artwork	UPC code
Deposit or advance	Shipping
Printing labels	

Promotional Expenses	
Promotional photo shoot and duplication	Launch party
	Internet ads
Events	Press kits, sample CDs
Posters	Postage
Advertising	

Tour Expenses (to be recouped from Artist Royalties)	
Bus	Wardrobe
Crew	Promotion
Food and lodging	Agent's cut
Fuel	Manager's cut
Consumable supplies	
TOTAL	
Add 30% for unexpected expenses, overruns and emergencies	

Pre-Production

The recording session in the studio isn't the first step in making an album—it comes after a lot of work. There is planning, scheduling, and organizing that goes on before the artist even gets to the studio. Remember what Benjamin Franklin (and your parents) said: "If you fail to plan, you plan to fail." Every hour spent in the studio costs money. The artist and staff members need to be ready to go to work and then work hard so nobody is wasting money.

The administrative tasks

The record label finds and books a studio and a sound engineer, hires a producer (some contract say the artist does this), and make sure everyone has signed a contract. Everyone needs to sign any tax documents that are needed. Licenses are needed to use any copyrighted music or lyrics.

> ♫ **FAST FACT**
>
> Musicians, sound engineers, and other technicians may belong to a trade union that sets payment guidelines and sets standards for working conditions.

Each person needs to understand his or her responsibilities before recording. Equipment and supplies need to be bought or rented, and don't forget transportation, lodging, and catering during the recording session. Try not to forget any detail. Everyone needs a production calendar to stay on track, filled with rehearsal times and any meetings that may need to happen.

The artist's preparation

The artist and the record label choose the songs for the album. The artist should practice as much as possible. Any backup musicians need to also work out their parts in advance. The artist should practice performing while standing since that's how he or she will be recording. Make sure everyone has the musical instruments they need, including extra guitar strings, backup equipment, etc. The artist—and everyone else—needs to remember to get plenty of rest the night before the recording session.

The meeting with producer, engineer and artist

The recording engineer, producer, artist, and anyone else necessary should meet to talk about the recording session. The engineer needs a rough copy of the album so he or she will know what to expect. If possible, the engineer should hear a live performance of the artist.

The communication channels

Everyone needs to talk! The artist and producer need to be on the same page as far as plans and expectations—and about money. For example, there may be a goal of recording three songs per day for four days. The money saved during the recording session can go toward promoting the new record. The better you understand each other, the more smoothly you will be able to work together.

There should be some rules so nobody gets distracted (like phone calls and friends stopping by) during the recording session, and make sure everyone understands them. Be on time every day, and don't take long coffee breaks and lunch breaks. Basically, if you act professionally, you will be seen as a professional—even if you're young.

Picking Out a Studio

Recording studios are everywhere. A recording studio can be anything from someone's garage or bedroom to a nice setup with several sound rooms. Equipment, services, and prices vary widely from one studio to another. With modern equipment and computer software, a good sound engineer can record a good-quality album for $10,000 to $20,000. Yet a recording session at one of the top studios in New York or California could cost more than $100,000. The recording studio will have a lot to do with how good your final product ends up being, so find the one that is a good fit for your vision—and your wallet. Remember: you want a studio and staff that can help you succeed not only with this record, but also with your future records, too.

You can find local recording studios on the internet, and by talking with local musicians, music stores, DJs, and entertainment lawyers, as well as reading through the ads in music fan magazines. If you strike out at one studio, ask the person to suggest others. Post an ad on Craigslist (**www.craigslist.org**). Talk to people at local universities and technical schools that teach media classes. Look in directories such as the Musicians Atlas (**www.musiciansatlas.com**) or RecordProduction.com (**www.record production.com/usa_studio_website_directory.htm**). If you like the quality of your artist's demo, ask where it was recorded.

Make a list of the best prospects, what their services are, and how much they cost. Visit the studios on your list, talk to the owners and engineers, and ask to see their equipment. Bring along your producer or someone with experience recording to help you evaluate the studio.

QUESTIONS TO ASK AT THE STUDIO

- Do you provide a sound engineer for what I'm paying?

- Can I hear samples of the engineer's work?

- Can I watch a recording session to see for myself how the engineer works with the musicians?

- How many microphones are used?

- What amplifiers or instruments are available in the studio?

- Do you have the equipment to make a final master recording?

- What musicians have recorded at the studio?

- Can I listen to their records?

- Can I contact them to learn how they feel about their experience recording in that studio?

Bring your list down to three or four possible studios. While you're deciding which to choose, think about these things:

- Do you feel comfortable in the studio environment?

If the studio or the engineer intimidates you or makes you feel nervous, follow your intuition and walk away. Is the recording area large enough to fit the artist and backup musicians? Do you like the sound of the room? Both artist and producer should visit the studio and give his or her opinion.

- Does the studio have the equipment you need?

Every style of music uses different instruments and equipment. Make sure the studio has the right equipment for your artist and that the engineer is experienced with your genre.

- Does the price fit your budget?

Renting a studio will eat up a large part of your budget, but it's not your only expense. If you spend more than you planned for the recording, you won't have enough money for publicity later. There are some ways to talk down the price. Some studios give discounts if you book for 24-hour blocks or for "graveyard" blocks (during the night and early morning hours—but remember that nobody is at his or her best when tired). You can also limit time spent in the recording studio by using another location for your practice time, and saving pricy studio time for recording.

TRY OUT THE STUDIO

If you can't decide on a studio, arrange to have your artist record a single in each and compare the results. The recordings will probably be good enough to be used on the final album with a little adjustment, and you will be able to see which studio produces the best results for the artist.

THE PRODUCER'S ROLE

A producer is kind of like the boss. He or she watches over the artist, musicians, and technicians to create the music everybody wants. Producers help choose the songs and background singers, coach the artist in the studio, take charge of the recording sessions, watch the budget, and oversee mixing and mastering. Many producers are also musicians and may be part of recording or arranging the music.

An experienced producer is super important to have and can make the difference between a "meh" album and a mega hit. The producer has a vision of the finished product and knows the steps needed to get there. The producer also helps keep everyone on schedule and focused, and he or she solves any problems that come up. He or she might know people in the music business to work with the artist and help make the record awesome. Producers work with many different artists and audiences, and—we hope—know what will appeal to the artist's audience.

The producer's contract

The Artist's Agreement talks about who hires the producer and the exact royalties the producer will earn. A lawyer should come up with a contract that says exactly what jobs the producer will do for the record and for the artist. Both sides will want to get this in writing *before* the recording starts.

Everyone involved in making a recording shares the copyright to that recording. The contract should transfer the producer's recording copyrights to the record label. Otherwise, the producer is actually a co-author of the music and can legally get a share of all the profits, not just royalties.

A producer who composes and records tracks to accompany an artist's vocals owns the rights to the written song. The producer should then get a credit in the song (his or her name is given as a co-author) and half the songwriting royalties. If a producer makes a major change in the song, he or she may be legally named as a co-author of the song and co-owner of the publishing rights. The producer's contract should tell clearly if the label has the right to use the producer's name in promoting the record.

♫ FAST FACT

During the Great Depression, the company that would become Sony Music Holdings bought up many record labels at bargain prices, including American Columbia Phonograph Company and its subsidiary Okeh Records, and gained control of their music catalogues.

Make sure a payment plan is included in the producer's contract, or the contract could be easy to void in the future, which would allow the producer to have rights to the recordings and even more money from the record label.

THE RECORDING ENGINEER'S ROLE

The recording engineer works the sound equipment during recording. Engineers should prepare by studying the artist's songs in advance, so they can help create the right sound. He or she listens to the audio, adjusts the equipment and recording levels, and sometimes coaches the artist so that the recording sounds perfect. The engineer makes sure all the studio equipment and instruments are set up, and that it all works, and is ready to go when the recording session begins.

The engineer should have expert knowledge of microphones, musical instruments, and amplifiers, as well as know about all the recording equipment in the studio and how they add to or change the music when it's recorded. Most studios will have an engineer used to their equipment. If you're using your own engineer, make sure he or she has time to practice with the studio equipment before recording starts. Either way, once again, make sure the jobs to be done and the money to be given are written out in a contract.

Mixing

During recording, the sounds of each instrument and each voice are re-corded—either one at a time or at the same time—onto several separate tracks that can each be changed to make them just what you want. Any track, such as the guitar part, that needs to be changed can be replaced with a re-recording. After all the tracks have been recorded, they must be mixed so that all of the tracks are heard at the right volume.

Mixing is just as important to the quality of a record as the recording of the music itself. While it may be tempting to rush the mixing if you're excited about the finished product, it should be done with great care and reviewed numerous times. Often several mixes are created before the recording is all the way done.

In a smaller studio, the mixing might be done by the recording engineer or by the producer, but in a larger studio there is a special mixing engineer. Usually the engineer and producer create a rough mix first, and then call in the artist and other musicians to review it and give their opinions.

The mix may sound different on the studio's high-quality speakers than it does on other sound systems. Make copies of the mix and play it on com-puters, boom boxes, MP3 players, and car stereos to see how it sounds. After listening to music for hours on end, you may lose the ability to hear the tiny things that make big differences. Take a break to rest your ears, and then listen again. Play the music for other people and listen to what they say. After the producer OKs the final mix, the tracks are all put into a single recording and the record is ready for mastering.

MASTERING

Mastering is the process of putting the recording into a data storage device (the master) where you will get all the copies of the music. Sometimes the recording studio will master your record, but in many cases, you will send it to a separate mastering studio. The cost for mastering will vary tremendously depending on the studio—Are they a large or small company? Are they well-established or starting out? What equipment do they use? The cost will also depend on your music—How many songs are on your album? How much work needs to be done? You might be able to master your record for as little as $500 or it may cost you $2,000 or more.

The mastering studio is different from the recording studio. There isn't a lot of furniture, and speakers are put around the room so the mastering engineer can listen without distractions. The songs are placed in order with blank space in between; volume is adjusted; clicks and buzzes are eliminated with noise reduction; and the very best quality is reached. The mastering engineer can't make changes to the individual tracks because they have already been combined into one recording. For CDs and digital files, the beginning and end of each song and an album index are set. The record is then transferred to a high-quality CD-R, a flash drive or external hard drive, or a digital format.

CASE STUDY: JOSH JONES

Experienced Freelance Sound
Engineer

What Does It Take to Make a Good Recording?

After helping several up-and-coming bands to record their first CDs, Jones has the following advice for an amateur musician or band who wants to make an album and sell it:

Make sure everyone, especially the drummer, can play to a click track. Missing takes costs money!

Know what you want before going into the studio. It's best to talk about the sound and feel of an album you are going for before you start.

Most importantly, BE REALISTIC about your expectations. Albums are not worth their price in gold like they used to be. The industry is changing . . . use your album more as a marketing tool, and get the fans on your side and out to your shows.

There are many aspects to making a good recording, such as the size and acoustic treatment of the room you are recording in. Walk around and listen to the room. Where does the sound start to liven up, where are all the low ends? Ultimately you need to rely on your ears — they won't lie to you.

Obviously the more high-end gear you can afford, the better. High-end converters, pre-amps, clocks and mics always help. Ultimately, a lot of a good recording lies with the engineer.

Are you micing the sweet spot of the instrument, which means placing the mic in the best location to capture the sound of the instrument? If you are using more than one mic, are you phasing? Are you in tune, and do you have the right tone?

Always use a DI (Direct Input) in line with stringed instruments, which is a cable that feeds the sound from an electric guitar directly into the recording device. I can't tell you how important this can be in the mixing process. If the take is good but the recording just doesn't cut it, you saved the mix just by doing this simple step.

Create samples of your drums for mixing later.

Take your time and get a useable take. Unless you are going for a special effect, Auto-Tune can't fix slop. Get the take as close as possible and use Auto-Tune as a tweaking tool to make it right.

Editing is probably the most overlooked aspect of a good recording. Make sure everything is on time. If you double your guitars, make sure they are in time with each other. Cut out excess noise.

Sound replacing your drums is pretty common. Using the samples you created in tracking will give you your clean, realistic drum sound.

Getting a good mix and mastering engineer is priceless. Knowing what frequencies to cut and how to niche your instruments to sit in the mix — and how to pan everything to get a good stereo image — is priceless. It is an art that takes many engineers years to master.

The cost of recording an album and having it mixed and mastered really does vary. I suppose with the bare minimum, the artist could buy his or her own interface and mics, and then record for relatively cheap. This is perfectly fine, but don't expect to get the same result as having high-end converters, pre's, and mics in line, not to mention the knowledge of an experienced engineer. This is a tough question to answer just because of the vast number of routes one could take. There are a lot of small pro-sumer (professional equipment for amateurs) grade studios popping up just because of how cheap some gear has become. Also, with plugins you can avoid buying high end outboard gear, again cutting the costs.

To locate an affordable recording studio, call around and ask your fellow musicians where they recorded. Many studios offer deals from time to time when they are slow. Just keep a look out. Remember going cheap is not always the best way either. Do your research . . . find out what kind of gear they have and whom the engineer has worked with (ask for a sample), and weigh the costs.

I have learned that being patient goes a long way in the studio. When you get nervous or agitated, so does the artist. If you make it a relaxed environment, the artist will get to the end product much faster, and will be more prone to want to work with you again.

Always back up your files, and keep the raw takes until you are sure they are no longer needed.

Every engineer hears differently. Don't be afraid to try new things, and create your own sound. Again, your ears won't lie to you.

I think the opportunity to get exposure through social networking sites like Facebook and YouTube is definitely there, but it depends greatly on the artist. The infrastructure is in place. With iTunes you can buy per track—anyone with an account can log in and download your music. So, talking distribution, you can get your music out to a large audience. However, this does not change the fact that you still have to do your marketing. Be unique with your marketing, use tools like YouTube, and see if you can get a video to go viral.

As I mentioned before, give your music away and get the fans to your shows. The industry is changing—the days of sitting back and selling albums have long been gone. Be proactive, be unique, and please have a live presence to back it up!

MANUFACTURING

Once your recording is done, you're ready to sell your record as a CD, vinyl record, or digital download. To sell digital downloads, you upload the files through the internet to a digital distribution channel. CDs and vinyl records must be made, packaged, and shipped to stores and customers. Some people use small local companies and some use global all-in-one companies that do it all, including printing the labels and posters, accounting, and the taking care of royalties and copyrights.

Someone will need to do this work. It takes time to make CDs once the master has been given to the company; you need to make sure the CDs will be ready when you need them to launch your new release. The manufacturer needs time to plan the production of your CDs. Knowing how much this will all cost will help you figure out how much to charge for the finished product and add up how much money you can expect from sales.

Look on the internet for a manufacturer so comparing prices and services is fast and easy. Talk to other artists, DJs, and people who work at record stores. If you like a CD, see what company made them. When you find a few that seem to fit what you're looking for, call them and ask about their prices. Ask them about how they make the products, how long it will take to deliver your order, and what formats they need for artwork and audio files. Some companies do all the work themselves on-site, including labels, and others hire people to do the work for them.

♫ FAST FACT

Psy's music video of "Gangnam Style" has almost three billion views. But superstar Adele's hit "Hello" got to one billion views faster than Psy's video had — she was at one billion views 88 days after uploading the video. It took Psy's video 159 days (**www.guinness worldrecords.com**).

Several companies such as CD Baby (**http://members.cdbaby.com**) and CreateSpace (**www.createspace.com**) let you manufacture and sell CDs and vinyl records on-demand; each time a customer orders a CD, it is created, packaged, and shipped. If you are a solo artist or a new band testing the waters with a limited budget, an all-in-one company might be the best solution. You will pay more for each CD, but the details like printing and shipping are taken care of for you. You can order a small number of CDs to begin with and get larger quantities later to place in retail outlets. Some of these companies will make a free sample of your CD so you can check it out first.

If you need boxes of CDs to sell at live events or if your distributer wants hundreds of CDs or vinyls to place in stores, find a CD manufacturer who will make and package them for you at a lower price. You can have CDs manufactured for less than $1 each, if you have the artwork already designed to be imprinted on the CDs. Bulk CDs without packaging cost even less — but you have to take care of the packaging yourself, of course.

Some manufacturers will give you a CD to review and approve before running your full order. Others charge extra for sample CDs. It is important to get samples and listen to your CD several times before you go ahead with the having them made. Ask the artist and producer to listen, too. You don't want to make a thousand CDs and then find something wrong.

Duplication and replication

Duplication means making CDs using CD burners, kind like the one in your personal computer. Hundreds of CDs are copied at the same time on linked computers, each with several CD/DVD trays. In replication, they use a glass master — a circular glass block about 240 mm in diameter and six mm deep with a special chemical coating. The information on the master recording is engraved on the face of the glass master, which is then used to press the recording into the plastic CDs as they are made. The artwork on duplicated CDs isn't usually as good as the silk-screening on replicated CDs. Duplicated CDs are just fine, but replicated discs have better quality.

If your first run will be less than 1,000 copies, you'll probably have them duplicated. Most manufacturers won't do a replication order for fewer than one thousand CDs; it's expensive unless you're creating a large number.

Artwork and labels

Digital downloads and CDs *and* vinyl records all need graphics. An image will appear on the CD case, the cover of the vinyl record, and the sales page for the digital download. This image needs to make a good first impression. Fans see the image, and then think of the songs on the album. If you don't have a talented friend who does graphics, hire a professional—or even an art student. You can use a good photo of the artist on the cover, but if the artist is not already famous, it might not attract people to buy it. Fans might not like the artist's clothes, image, or looks; if the image doesn't fit the genre, a potential fan might choose to buy another artist's CD. It is safer to use the name of the album, the name of the artist, and some basic information about the band. The colors, font, and images should fit with the genre and tell you something about the music.

It's your choice what words to put on the CD or record label: a list of the songs, a bio of the artist, a statement from the artist, or nothing at all. Be sure to include the name of the record label, its logo, and contact information such as the website or address. Also, include the © symbol and the words "Copyrighted 20__."

JUDGING A CD BY ITS COVER

Your CD has a certain sound, in a certain genre. You want people who like that kind of music to buy your CD. Catch their attention by your packaging — but don't get too crazy. Some might make a CD package an unusual shape or odd size. That makes it hard for a store to fit the CDs in a regular display rack — or put the CDs in those plastic cases to prevent them being stolen. (More than two-thirds of all music stores use some kind of security tag or case.) A register can't scan a CD without a barcode. If your CD will be sold in a store, print the album's title or band's name on the top half of the label so everyone can see it easily when they're browsing through the racks. Unique packaging might sell better at live performances.

The graphics on your CD label or vinyl record cover will need to be a certain way for the printing company, so keep that in mind. Most printing companies will share templates and instructions on their websites. Talk with the printing company in advance so there's won't be any mistakes that might cause delays. Make sure you look at the finished artwork carefully for spelling errors; ask two or three people to look at it in case you miss something.

If artwork is printed directly onto a CD, it is typically screen-printed and has a coarser resolution. If the design is too complicated, it might not look right on the CD. A better bet is a simpler design in one or two colors that has the same theme as your CD label.

Some CD manufacturers have your labels printed as part of the job. If you are using a separate company for printing, plan ahead so the labels are shipped to the CD manufacturer on time. Keep your timeline in mind as you plan. A graphic artist needs enough time to create a design, submit it, and make any changes before the labels are printed.

UPC Bar Code

You know that series of black lines and numbers scanned at the cash register when someone buys an item? It's a UPC bar code, and you need one on your cover to sell it. Bar codes let stores to keep track of merchandise and automatically enter prices into their cash registers. In the music industry, bar codes are important because they're used by Nielsen SoundScan, the official method of tracking sales of music and music video products. From cash registers to online stores and digital music services, SoundScan is the data source for the *Billboard* music charts; without a bar code, your record will never appear on the charts.

If you have less than 100 items, you can get a bar code ID is about $750 for an independent record label, plus an annual renewal of $150. You can register online at GS1 (**www.gs1us.org**). You can use a software program such as SmartCode (**www.technoriversoft.com/products.html**) to make bar codes for your labels. If you're not ready for your own bar code, you can get one from a third party. Some CD manufacturers give you a free bar code for your CD using their own registration ID numbers; others charge you $25 to $50.

Every record has a catalog number, three letters followed by three numbers, such as "XYZ123." It needs to be somewhere on your CD label so employees of the stores can see it when they're helping customers find music or restocking CDs.

BAR CODES CAN BE ADDED LATER

If you don't put a bar code on your CDs at first and then decide you need one, you can always get one later. The bar code can be printed on stickers to be affixed to your CD covers.

How many to make?

The number of CDs and records you will have made for your first order of CDs will depend on the marketing plan and budget. Some stores may require a specific number. If you plan to sell CDs at live performances, a few hundred will be enough. The cost per CD may be lower if you order a larger quantity; in that case, buy as many as you can afford because your profit on each one will be higher. If the manufacturer is able to get you more CDs within a few days, you can order a small amount at first and later order more if you start to sell out.

Giveaways

You'll be giving away free promotional CDs to DJs, radio stations, music critics, distributors, and fans. Add up how many you need for this and ask the manufacturer not to shrink-wrap them in plastic; you can save a little money that way. Promotional copies should be marked as "promos" in some way. Otherwise, someone could return one to a distributor or music store for credit, and you'll be refunding them for a CD you gave away. Write "Promo" across the label, punch a hole in the bar code, or cut corners off the label to indicate they are not cleans—the name for product sold in stores.

♫ FAST FACT

The company that would become EMI was very successful from the late 1950s to the early 1970s, with pop and rock artists including Frank Sinatra, Cliff Richard, The Shadows, The Beach Boys, The Hollies, Cilla Black, and Pink Floyd. And you might know this name: the Beatles, now estimated to have sold more than one billion records, were signed by EMI in 1962.

VINYL IS BACK, BABY!

Cassette tapes all but disappeared from store shelves in 2007, and digital downloads sell way better than CDs, but vinyl records are making a comeback. They may never dominate the music industry again, but the market for them is growing. According to Fortune.com, vinyl record sales were up 32 percent in 2015, at $416 million, the highest level since 1988.

Most vinyl albums are sold by independent record stores. Although owners of fine stereo systems insist the sound of a vinyl album is far better than a CD or digital file, records are being bought mostly by people in their 20s and 30s. They appear to be attracted by the packaging and accompanying literature and by the collectability of vinyl albums. Popular vinyl albums are mostly re-issued classics and indies, although newer artists like Justin Bieber and Taylor Swift have had limited editions of their new releases on vinyl in recent years.

Recordings are mastered differently for vinyl records because too much bass can cause the phonograph needle to jump out of the groove on the record. If you want to make a vinyl record, you will probably have to pay for two mastering sessions.

CHAPTER 6

Publishing

Publishing rights to music makes a label a lot of money. Publishing rights bring in about one-third of a record label's profits. Every recorded song has two copyrights: one for the sound recording and one for the words and music. Music publishing handles these copyrights. In 2016 in the U.S., whoever owns these rights gets a mechanical royalty of 9.1 cents for each physical record or download sold, and 10.5 percent from streaming the song over the internet for subscription or ad-based services.

Music is used so many ways through new technologies and media. TV commercials used to have their own jingles; now many use hit songs to catch the viewer's attention. Many TV shows use well-known songs for theme songs or play top hits during the shows. Songs are used in internet ads and greeting cards, and in video games and arcade games, in clothing stores and supermarkets. You hear songs while you're on hold calling a business. Songs are sung in talent competitions and played on karaoke machines. For any of these uses, you need a mechanical license. Publishers also sell sheet music and lyrics to choirs, orchestras, and high school bands.

MUSIC PUBLISHING IS BIG BUSINESS

Bug Music Inc. has copyrights for more than 250,000 songs including the songs "Fever," "What a Wonderful World," and "Happy Together." In October of 2010, it acquired the Saban Music Group catalog, which includes theme music from cartoons like "Mighty Morphin Power Rangers" and "Teenage Mutant Ninja Turtles." Bug Music collects money every time one of its songs is downloaded or sold as part of a CD and money from streaming its songs over the internet. The company makes even more money by licensing its songs for use in TV commercials, films, video games, and digital greetings cards. In 2011, Bug Music brought in sales of around $80 million. That same year, Bug was bought by BMG for $300 million! Buying Bug Music was a great investment; along with money made after buying out other smaller companies and artists, BMG is on track to make $500 million in revenue in 2016!

It's no good having a song if nobody knows about it. (We'll look at publicity in Chapter 10: Promotion and Marketing.) Some independent labels promote their artists' songs themselves. Others give part of their rights to another music publisher and share the mechanical royalties, known as co-publishing. The label can still get some money from music publishing, and the co-publisher does the marketing. Even if the royalty on one song is only a few cents, if that song becomes a hit, that can mean a lot of money.

NON-EXCLUSIVE SONGWRITER AGREEMENT

Usually, the songwriter and the publisher share publishing royalties equally. However, in a non-exclusive songwriter agreement, the songwriter gives all the publishing rights to the publisher and keeps the songwriter royalties. (This is different from mechanical licenses or video licenses, which are always split between the songwriter and publisher, and performing royalties, where everyone gets his or her own separate share.)

In a non-exclusive songwriter agreement, the songwriter promises the song is original —no one else will say that he or she helped write it. This means the songwriter has to pay any legal expenses if someone sues the publisher over the copyright. It happens sometimes that a band member gets mad and later says he or she helped write a hit song. The publisher also has the right to take to court anyone who violates the copyright.

HOW DO YOU GET PAID FROM THESE ROYALTIES?

In the U.S., the Harry Fox Agency (**www.harryfox.com**), gives out mechanical licenses and collects the royalties when records and digital downloads are sold. The music publisher is supposed to pay the songwriter his or her half of the royalty money.

Now that streaming is so popular, subscription digital download services (limited download) and services such as Napster and Rhapsody will pay a mechanical royalty of 10.5 percent of the money they make, minus anything owed for performance royalties. Royalty-free streaming is allowed in some cases for publicity.

BUT FIRST, YOU NEED A MUSIC PUBLISHING COMPANY

To get publishing royalties, you have to have a publishing company and a business bank account. Even a songwriter who is self-publishing needs an account to get the publisher's half of the royalties. To open a publishing company, you first send in three choices of business names to ASCAP, BMI, or SESAC—whichever you or your songwriter is affiliated with. If your songwriters are working with more than one of these agencies, you will have to open a company with each of them. The agency will check your name and make sure someone else is not using it. Once the name is approved, you get a business license and register your publishing company legally.

♫ FAST FACT

EMI's album sales declined with the rapid increase of digital downloads.

CO-PUBLISHING AGREEMENT

An unsigned artist may be willing to sign over the copyrights in order to get a record deal, but most artists want to keep at least some of their publishing rights. This is when a co-publishing agreement is used. The artist's publishing company owns the copyrights, and then that company gives part of the rights to the label's publishing company. The two publishers might split rights equally, or one may take a larger part. (Remember—this is only for the publisher's half of the royalties; the songwriter keeps all of those royalties. So, if you have 50 percent of the publishing royalties, you only get 25 percent of the total royalties.) This deal works well when two or more songwriters who worked together on a song but have different publishers, or if two publishers want to share the rights to a song. Both publishers own part of the copyright and promote the song, but only one, known as "the Company," does the administrative work and handles the royalties.

A co-publishing agreement is usually a good idea for both sides: the more experienced publisher, usually the record label, makes sure the behind-the-scenes-work is done right, while the less-experienced artist/songwriter still gets paid and catches people's attention for the song by performing it.

EXCLUSIVE SONGWRITER AGREEMENT

In an Exclusive Songwriter Agreement, a songwriter signs over the rights to his or her songs in exchange for a steady paycheck. It is something like an employment contract and is used mostly for songwriters who don't perform the songs. The contract is only for a certain time frame, but rights to the songs still belong to the publisher after the contract ends. The publisher usually can change the songs if he or she wants to. The songwriter allowed to write songs for anyone else during the contract.

ADMINISTRATION AGREEMENT

Instead of handing the copyrights to his or her songs over to the record label's publisher, an artist/songwriter who likes to bargain might let the publisher take care of the rights and then get a part of the royalties. The publisher handles all the registration and administrative details, gives licenses, collects and pays royalties, and even can go to court for the artist if needed. Basically, the songwriter is paying the publisher to do the behind-the-scenes work.

LICENSING

A song belongs to the songwriter or the publisher and can't be used by anyone without a license. A license gives permission to use a song—play it, re-record it, use it in a movie or TV show, print the lyrics in a book, sample it, perform it onstage, or make a music video for it. Each use needs a different kind of license.

A mechanical license gives a record label permission to copy a song and distribute it. Under U.S. copyright law, once a song has been published for the first time, mechanical licenses are compulsory. Any record company can get a mechanical license, whether the publisher wants to grant it or not, by filing a notice with the U.S. Copyright Office. Most publishers are fine with licensing their songs.

Each license can only be used for one thing, and then separate licenses are needed to use the song again. You might get a license to record a song, but then you need a separate license to use that song in a video game or a commercial. You pay the regular mechanical royalty rate, unless the publisher and record label make a deal for a lower rate.

A videogram license is to make a music video. A synchronization license allows that video to be shown on TV or in a movie. Sometimes these are combined in a single license. However, if the publisher refuses to grant the license, the video cannot be filmed.

Any company that wants to use the recorded version of a song needs to get the master use license from the record label. Before using the song, however, the company also needs a mechanical license from the publisher. In this case, both the artist and the songwriter will earn their separate royalties.

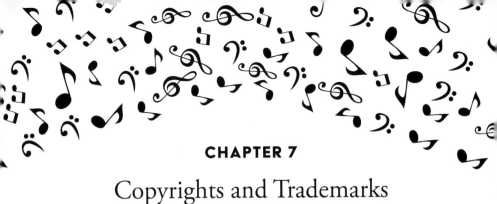

CHAPTER 7

Copyrights and Trademarks

The music industry is all about copyrights for recorded and written songs and the brands and images that go along with a label and its artists. Copyright means legal protection promised in the U.S. Constitution and given by law for original work. A copyright gives the owner the exclusive right to make copies, license, and otherwise exploit a literary, musical, or artistic work in printed, audio, or video form.

COPYRIGHT

You don't have to register a copyright to protect your work, or even have it officially published; it's under copyright protection the moment it is created. But you still need to register with the U.S. Copyright Office if you ever have a court case against someone who is using your work without permission.

In the music industry, there are two types of authors: songwriters and recording artists. A songwriter's work is copyrighted the moment the song is written down or recorded. A recording artist owns a recorded performance as soon as the recording is made.

Copyrights for written songs aren't the same as copyrights for the recordings of those songs. A publishing company gets the copyright for a written song through a publishing agreement, and a record label needs a recording agreement before going to the studio. The songwriter gets the mechanical royalty, and the recording artist gets a performance royalty each time the recording is sold. A third party wanting to use the recording in a movie or a commercial must pay both the publisher and from the record label.

How long does a copyright last?

In the U.S., a work that was made on or after January 1, 1978 is automatically protected from that moment on, until the author's death plus an additional 70 years after that. If two or more people wrote it together, the term lasts for 70 years after the last author's dies.

If an artist was hired to create a work, or if the author isn't known or named (unless the author's identity is somewhere in Copyright Office records), copyrights last 95 years from when the work was published or 120 years from when it was created, whichever is shorter.

Copyright registration

Nobody *has* to get a copyright. But you might want to. Here's why:

- Registration leaves a public record that your work is yours.

- Before you can take someone to court for breaking copyright, it has to be registered.

- If you register within five years of publishing, registration gives evidence in court that your copyright is valid.

- If you register within three months after publishing the work or before someone broke the copyright, statutory damages (money *could* have made) and attorney's fees can be given to the copyright owner in court. Otherwise, only the actual damages and profits can be paid.

- Registration lets you record the registration with U. S. Customs so your music can't be taken and sold in another country. Check this out at the U. S. Customs and Border Protection website: **https:// apps.cbp.gov/e-recordations**.

How do I file a copyright?

An application for copyright registration needs three things: a completed application form, a nonrefundable filing fee, and a "deposit" that won't be returned—meaning a copy of the work being registered. A copyright registration starts on the date the copyright office receives these, no matter how long it takes to process the application and mail the registration certificate.

Can I do it online?

You can register online for copyrights for books; art; performing arts works, including movies; sound recordings; and singles. Registering online gives you a lower filing fee, fastest processing time, and you can track your application, pay your fee online, and even upload certain deposits as electronic files. You can still register online and save money even if you have to send in a hard-copy deposit. You can find out more at the copyright office website at **www.copyright.gov** — click on "electronic copyright office."

♫ FAST FACT

The U.S. Copyright Office was founded in 1870.

COPYRIGHT NOTICE

You don't have to have a copyright notice on your CD's label under U.S. law, though it is often a good idea. You don't even have to have permission from the copyright office or have finished your copyright registration with them.

What should a copyright look like?

The visual part of your copyright needs three things:

1. The symbol © (the letter C in a circle), the word "Copyright," or the abbreviation "Copr."

2. The year the work was first published.

3. The name of the owner of copyright in the work, or an abbreviation of the name.

Example: © 2018 John Doe.

The © notice is used only on things you can physically see. Certain kinds of works—like music, plays, and books—may be fixed not in "copies," but by means of a sound recording. Because sound recordings like tapes and CDs are "phonorecords" and not "copies," the © notice is not used.

What does a Phonorecords right look like?

The visual record for phonorecords needs three things:

1. The symbol ℗ (a letter P in a circle).

2. The year the work was first recorded.

3. The name of the owner of copyright in the work, or an abbreviation of the name. If the producer's name is on the phonorecord label, and if no other name is listed, the producer's name is used.

Example: ℗ 2008 A.B.C. Records Inc.

Where should these go?

The copyright notice be in an obvious place on the package. The three things listed in the notice should go together on the copies or phonorecords or on the label or container.

TRADEMARKS

A trademark is a word, phrase, symbol, or design, or a combination of these, that sets you apart from others. You don't have to register a trademark; it's real because you use it. To protect the money invested into your music career, it's wise to register your trademarks in the Principal Register of the U.S. Patent and Trademark Office (USPTO). You don't want a copy-cat band stealing your name after you have made it famous.

♫ **FAST FACT**

The first CD player was released by Sony in 1982 (**www.pcworld .com**).

Just like registering a copyright, having a trademark registration benefits you:

- Registration shows everyone you own the mark and gives proof of your ownership in court.

- You can't go to court over the trademark unless it's been registered.

- You can use the U.S registration to register your work in foreign countries.

- You can file with U.S. Customs to protect your music in case someone is misusing it in another country.

You can use the ™ (trademark) or ᔆᴹ (service mark) whether or not you have filed an application with the USPTO. However, you can't use the federal registration symbol ® until *after* your trademark registration is completely done. You can learn more about registering a trademark or a service mark on the USPTO website (**www.uspto.gov/trademarks/basics/Basic _Facts_Trademarks.jsp**).

CHAPTER 8

Distribution — Getting the Music Out There

Getting your music out where fans can buy it is the name of the game of distribution. Music sold as digital downloads or MP3 files is distributed through music sales websites on the internet. CDs and vinyl records must be physically shipped from the manufacturer to record stores and retail outlets.

Distribution happens in different ways. Major labels are able to put their products in stores all over the world, all at the right time to synch with their marketing strategy. Your local distributors will act as a middleman, buying records from multiple record labels and placing them in retail stores nearby. Subdistributors called rack jobbers buy CDs, DVDs, and music merchandise wholesale and sell them in drugstores, bookstores, department stores, and other places that sell things other than music. One-stops are subdistributors that wholesale a wide selection of CDs, movies, games, and other media to smaller independent stores. These mom-and-pop stores often help create a grassroots interest in a new artist.

Sometimes manufacturers also will distribute, but you can also find all kinds of companies that will do the distributing for you, like getting your CD to stores, packing, shipping, and keeping track of the money (for a fee). Newbies in the music field probably start by distributing their own CDs, selling them at live performances, and visiting retail stores in their area.

Putting your CD on a shelf in a music store or on a website doesn't mean fans will buy it. Distribution companies get a commission for each record sold. But nobody will make money unless a good marketing strategy drums up a demand for your music. Distributors work closely with record labels and retailers on marketing efforts, making sure records are available where and when fans want to buy them.

We call the process that most people use to sell music "consignment"—the music goes on the shelves in a retail store, and you get paid only when it sells. Remember that you are competing for shelf space with thousands of other CDs. After a few weeks or months, if your records are not selling, the record store will give them back to make room on its shelves for other artists.

Your record label needs the money from record sales to pay for promotion and fund new projects. Money doesn't come pouring in right away, but will trickle in gradually over time as retail outlets sell CDs and handle their payments. Even when your record becomes an immediate hit, it will be weeks and even months before you receive payment from your retail outlets or distributors. In your marketing budget, plan for an active marketing campaign for several months before you start expecting record sales to pay your expenses. You might get money during this time from other sources, like live performance ticket sales or selling merchandise, but without awesome marketing, your record won't sell through retail outlets; without retail sales, your distributor won't pay you.

DO IT YOURSELF

When artists or record labels first start out, they probably do the distribution themselves. A large distributor won't be interested in brand new artists and records. Distribution companies pay their own expenses — salaries of salespeople, shipping, warehousing costs — and they need to make a profit. Distributors are looking for records they know will sell. Until you have shown that your music has steady sales and a strong fan base, you can't expect a big company to work for you.

You also might not want to work with a big company at first. Big distribution means big marketing, which means lots of money. Hiring a marketing agency is expensive, and you may never make back your costs. You also must make lots of albums for the distributor. Whether they sell or not, these CDs and records, and the money you paid in having them made them, will be sitting on store shelves for months. A large company has other artists to take care of, and may not give you the attention you want to have.

When your first shipment of one thousand CDs arrives on your doorstep, how are you going to sell them? Begin by selling CDs at your artists' live performances. Start with a launch party and take boxes of CDs to every place the artist performs. Set up a merchandise table by the door or near the stage. Either the artist or someone from the record label can be responsible for selling CDs. Maybe even a friend or family member can supervise the merchandise table. The artist should announce during the performance that CDs are available for sale. If possible, an artist should sit nearby during breaks to chat with fans and sign CDs or posters. Making a connection with the fans is important. Fans who are moved by the performance or want to support the artist will be inspired to buy a CD on the spot. If anyone doesn't want to buy right away, have a supply of one-sheets (see below) to hand out with information about the CD and where it can be purchased, for example, a website address or local store.

Be sure to keep track of the CDs sold at live performances; it is very easy for some to "disappear" during the excitement. Count CDs before and after each performance. If the artist is going to sell the CDs himself or herself, a good idea would be for the artist to buy some at a wholesale price. Then, the artist can keep the profit from the CDs he or she sells.

DON'T FORGET SALES TAX!

Remember: you're supposed to charge and pay sales tax when you sell the CDs. If you're making cash sales, you might want to adjust the price so the total comes out to an even dollar amount, such as $10 or $15.

Take the CDs to any store that might sell them: local record stores, bookstores, coffee shops, and art galleries. Ask the manager if he or she would be willing to take some CDs on consignment. Be friendly, and build a relationship with these stores. Play your CD for them and see if they like it. Listen to their advice. Salespeople in record stores often tell their customers about music they themselves find exciting. Ask to book a live performance where the music is being sold. If a store doesn't accept your CDs right away, don't give up. You might be more successful on a return visit or with future CDs. Once you have left a consignment, check in with the store at regular intervals to see if any CDs have been sold and if the store needs more. Of course, as you sell them, keep good records!

If you leave a consignment of records in a store, take along a receipt and get the record store manager's signature to sign off on how many CDs were left. The receipt will be super important when you're asking the store for payment later on.

Some manufacturers allow you to place orders online and have them shipped directly to anywhere. You can give retailers a login and a discount code to buy CDs directly at wholesale prices. A manufacturer who handles packing and shipping for you saves you a lot of work, so you will have more time for marketing.

♫ FAST FACT

You never know what's going to make a song the next hit single. The song "Dust in the Wind" by the progressive rock band Kansas sold more than a million units after becoming a hit single — and people still listen to it today, many years after its 1978 release. The song has a distinctive guitar line of fingerpicking — the songwriter, Kerry Livgren, had just been playing around on the guitar doing those finger exercises when his wife Vicci suggested turning them into a song.

MAKE YOUR ONE-SHEET AWESOME

A one-sheet is a single page sharing all the important information about the CD and the artist. You can make a glossy, full-color one-sheet and have it copied by a printer or an office supply store, but a black-and-white copy works too. The one-sheet should have the album name and the record label name, a short description of the music, bios of the members of the band, and contact information for the record label. You should have an image of the album cover and/or the artist. The one-sheet can also include press reviews, the artist's touring schedule and other information to get people excited. One-sheets for distributors and retail stores should also include the UPC code, release date, order information, catalog number, and what the CD price should be. Stores use the one-sheet to enter information about the CD into sales system.

> Give stores enough one-sheets to hand out to interested customers. If
> you are using a distributor, it will also need a large amount for its re-
> tailers. You can create a special one-sheet to hand out to fans at live
> performances, music festivals, and clubs, with information about how
> they can buy the album online.

When self-promotion starts to bring in a good amount of money, it may be time to think bigger. You might find places to sell the music in other parts of the state or country. If your online sales are doing well, you may be able to get your music album with some of the bigger names, like iTunes, if they weren't interested before.

SELLING YOUR MUSIC ONLINE

There are two ways online distribution happens: CDs and vinyl records (through online retailers) and digital music downloads. In 2015, out of all the music bought, 46 percent of it was downloaded, meaning that number is almost exactly the same as the number of times people bought a physical CD or record. Streaming is the fastest growing way to listen to music now — it counts for one-fourth of the online music sold.

Of course, people will still buy hard copies of records. Music fans not only enjoy listening to music, but also they apparently like to have CDs they can hold in their hands, give as gifts, buy as souvenirs, and collect. Selling CDs at live performances is still important for a young record label and a new artist trying to win over fans. Still, the internet has changed the way in which retail sales of CDs and vinyl records are conducted. People who buy a CD no longer go to big stores to look around; they do a quick online search and order it by mail from the cheapest place they can find. Small record stores, with staff who can share the latest artists and give personal attention to their customers, are still doing well.

There are a lot of advantages in online stales. It doesn't matter where they are; fans anywhere in the world can listen to and buy your music. All you have to do is get their attention. Artists use online communities and social networks, and friends tell each other about new artists from the comfort of their couches without ever meeting face-to-face or popping a CD into a CD player. A website can give information and sell merchandise, 24 hours a day, without anyone having to answer a telephone.

To sell music downloads, you don't have to invest any money in a physical product. The buyer downloads a file onto a computer, MP3 player, or other listening device, and the distributor gets paid when a sale is made. Just like sales in record stores, however, you need good marketing. Buyers usually purchase one song at a time instead of an entire album. You are competing with millions of other songs and hundreds of thousands of artists; you must find a way to reach your target audience and to stand out from the crowd. Touring and live performances will win fans, as well as through online videos, marketing, and social networking. After an artist goes to a university campus or a club or has music played on a local radio station, people will go online to check them out and maybe buy the music. Fans want to find the latest, greatest group, and then introduce it to their friends.

Online, fans can listen to short music samples before buying; interviews and live performances can also be streamed for free; free downloads, and ringtone sales can draw people in. Some artists offer free downloads of different versions of their songs. Customers can also buy merchandise by getting online.

Digital music downloads are also sold in "real" stores, like the kiosks in record stores where you can make a playlist and burn it to a CD or upload it on to an MP3 player. Digital music is also sold in coin-operated juke-boxes and as part of video arcade games.

Digital music sales

Digital music files are sold online, in different ways. Songs and albums are sold straight up as permanent digital downloads (Digital Phonorecord Deliveries, or DPDs) that you buy one time and then have forever—just like if you bought a CD in a record store. The sale of individual songs is sometimes called á la *carte* because the buyer picks and chooses only the songs he or she likes, rather than buying a whole album. Listeners can create playlists of their favorite songs, or of songs tied together by a certain theme.

Some music downloads can only be listened to on one device, like a computer or MP3 player. New laws and technology let the buyers make a few copies of the songs they bought for other devices ("to go" services), for example, on a laptop and an MP3 player. If you can listen to the song without being connected to the internet, that's called an untethered file.

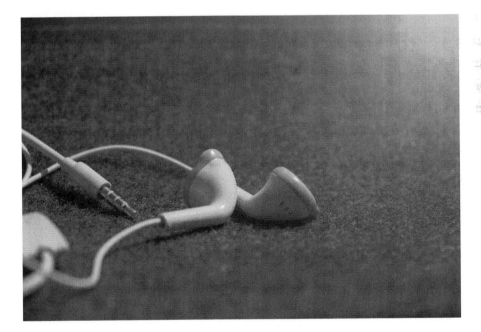

Subscription sites like eMusic (**www.emusic.com**) charge a monthly fee for a certain number of permanent downloads each month. Every month, you can add new songs to your playlist. But here's something to remember about sites like these: some subscription downloads are only yours as long as you're making monthly payments.

TALES FROM THE INDUSTRY: Upbeat Records

"Greatest Hits" Albums

In a world where music fans can create their own playlists and easily download the songs they want to listen to, albums of a band's most popular songs still sell well. Many, many artists have had success in marketing greatest hits albums. To appeal to fans, the CDs might have rare, unreleased music or unique packaging. Greatest hits albums also help new listeners "meet" artists they didn't before.

Because greatest hits albums sell so well, labels are pushing artists to make these records relatively early in their careers. Britney Spears, Hilary Duff, and Sugar Ray have already released "greatest hits" albums. Some artists, however, are against it. AC/DC, Radiohead, Phish, Pink Floyd, and Metallica are among the groups who refuse to break up their prior albums into individual "hits." They consider each of their albums as a work of art to be listened to as a whole.

Does a label have to have permission from a band to make a greatest hits album? That depends on the contract between them. There was big-time legal drama when Cake (creator of famous songs such as "The Distance" and "Short Skirt, Long Jacket") refused to make a greatest hits album for Columbia Records. The band thought it was too early for a "Best of Cake" CD because they had released only a few albums. Cake lead singer and guitarist John McCrea said the idea "reeks of desperation." Cake left Columbia to form its own label,

Upbeat Records, and in 2007, instead of a greatest hits album, it released "B-Sides and Rarities," a collection of covers including Black Sabbath's "War Pigs," Kenny Rogers's "Ruby, Don't Take Your Love to Town," and Barry White's "Never, Never Gonna Give You Up."

Over its twenty-year history, Cake proved it was above falling in line to trends and pressures of the music industry. The band follows its own ideals. Cake has recently built its own environmentally-friendly studio and says that being free from the demands of a large label gives it the time to refine its sound and make good-quality music.

DIGITAL RIGHTS MANAGEMENT (DRM) — SOUNDS LIKE ROCKET SCIENCE, BUT IT'S SO COOL!

Digital Rights Management (DRM) technology controls the use and sharing of music files and protects the artists and record labels so they get paid fairly. Each music file has rules tagged into its metafiles, like its price, how a buyer can access it, how many times it can be played, whether it can be saved or copied, and the time frame when it can be played. Individual licenses are handled for each person who buys the music file.

When a listener pays for the download, or subscribes to listen, he or she gets a license — a key to unlock the encryption and use the file. The license is delivered to a computer or listening device without the buyer even knowing. It may be delivered when the payment is made, when music is listened to, or each time the music is played. The listener can then use the music according to the rules in the file's meta-tag. In addition to making sure that people pay for the music they listen to, DRM technology tracks information like how many times a particular song is listened to. Awesome, right?

When you stream music on Rhapsody (**www.rhapsody.com**), MediaNet (**http://www.mndigital.com**), and Pandora (**www.pandora.com**), your music comes on-demand directly from the internet. Music files are up there in "the cloud," on the internet rather than in individual listening devices, and you get to them through an internet connection. You pay a monthly fee to listen to songs that they choose and place on a playlist on-line. Some streaming services like YouTube (**www.youtube.com**), Playlist.com (**www.playlist.com**), and MySpace (**www.myspace.com**) let fans listen to music for free and pay record labels some of the money they make by selling ads and commercials on their sites.

♫ FAST FACT

In 1994, the Warner publishing division, now Warner/Chappell Music, became the world's largest owner of song copyrights and the world's largest publisher of printed music when it purchased CPP/Belwin.

Non-interactive services, such as Pandora, Last.fm (**www.last.fm/music**), betterPropaganda (**www.betterpropaganda.com**), and Epitonic (**www.epitonic.com**), where the listener does not select the songs on the playlist, are treated as online radio stations. Some sites, such as Pandora, incorporate a discovery feature that searches for songs and genres that are like the songs the listener selects and plays them randomly. You can purchase each song through a link to iTunes or Amazon. Pandora also has a paid subscription for those of us who don't want to be interrupted by commercials.

There are still royalties and copyrights for streaming music. Streaming companies must sign license agreements with the music performance rights societies, BMI (**www.bmi.com**), ASCAP (**www.ascap.com**), and SESAC (**www.sesac.com**), to share the music. How much they pay is set by the

U.S. Copyright Office and by law, and they work out deals to pay record labels for using and selling the music.

HOW TO KNOW IF MUSIC LAWS HAVE CHANGED

Changes are always being made to music laws; you can find the latest information on the SoundExchange website (**www.sound exchange.com**), the Digital Media Association website (**www.dig media.org**), and the Copyright Royalty Board (**www.loc.gov/crb**).

When people buy ringtones for cell phones, digital downloads, and over-the-air soundtracks (OTAs) and audio streaming to mobile devices such as the Android and iPhone is even more complicated because a third party, the phone or wireless service carrier, is involved.

What's an aggregator, and what does he or she do?

When you think of a place to buy music online, you probably think of Amazon, iTunes, or Rhapsody (now Napster). Did you know there are more than 400 other companies like these? With so many ways to buy music, and thousands of record labels putting out music, who has the time to get the music to the right sources so they can be sold? That's where an aggregator comes in—basically a middleman with a digital "warehouse" of music and the ability to take care of the licensing part of getting the music out.

The major aggregators include The Orchard (**www.theorchard.com**), CD Baby (**www.cdbaby.com**), TuneCore (**www.tunecore.com**), and BFM Digital (**www.bfmdigital.com**)

You usually sign an exclusive deal with an aggregator for a term of one to three years. They get about 15 percent of the total sales revenue, which pays them to encode and format your music files, deliver them to music service providers, get the receipts, and pay you regularly. Some might make and distribute CDs too, do graphic design, make web pages, do some marketing, and even make posters and promo materials. Since people pay for digital downloads right away, aggregators are much better at paying you quickly and giving sales reports than a company that is physically selling your CDs or records (see below). You will, on average, be paid within two months of the time when a download was sold. Every contract is different, so pay attention to the details (and make sure you're not completely giving over the rights entirely to the aggregator).

FINDING A DISTRIBUTOR

An artist or a small record label might start off with self-distribution — and that's just fine — but there comes a time when you will need a distributor to expand your business to the next level. A distributor buys CDs (and vinyl records) from a record label and wholesales them to retail stores. They work with lots of retail outlets and know which seasons have the strongest sales, how to get people's attention in stores, and how to get store employees promoting and selling the records. Distributors make their money because they buy CDs at about 50 percent off and then charge the record stores a markup of $2 to $6 on each CD.

Finding a good distributor is the fastest way to get your CD on store shelves, but as mentioned in the beginning of this chapter, it is important to choose wisely. The distributor, record label, and artist work together to promote and sell a record. The distributor takes care of the physical aspects of selling records, the label works on marketing and drawing public attention to the artist, and the artist attracts customers through performances and being talked about in the media. When an artist has an interview on the radio, the distributor makes sure that listeners will be able to find the CD in stores.

Some distributors are really organized and pay the artist and labels on time. Others may disappoint you. Start looking for a distributor by chatting with the staff at stores where you sell your CDs and to other local artists. You can ask distributors exactly what services they provide and talk to some of their clients and retail outlets. It is wise to check on the internet by typing their name in a search engine to see if they are named in any lawsuits or if anyone is blogging complaints about them.

You'll be looking for a distributor who will do these things:

- Make sure your record is in stores in time for a planned release, publicity event, or a concert in the area.

- Get more music to stores when they start to run out of your records.

- Suggest promotional ideas, such as paying extra to have your CDs on an endcap (the display shelf at the end of an aisle) at a listening station in record stores; or having an in-store appearance by the artist.

- Share items like as one-sheets, cardboard stands to be placed near the register, posters, and fliers advertising live performances by the artist.

- Put your label in its catalog and its newsletters to stores that sell music.

- Organize ads in magazines and newspapers with other record labels or with stores.

- Collect money when music is sold and pay you.

Some distributors are huge and get music sold worldwide. Some are independent distributors and work on a regional level. All distribution companies are partners in some way with online music sales. Some of the digital music distribution companies also can sell your CDs in retail stores. When you are looking at distributors, find out what this means. Many distributors ask you to sign a contract that says you can only sell your CDs through them.

Here's what a distributor needs from *you*:

- One-sheets (remember those?) that include publicity plans, prices, tour schedules, release dates, and other important info.

- Some free CDs to be given away at stores, and promotional copies to be used by sales staff and handed out to the media.

- One-sheets and promo packages for retail outlets, and press kits for the media.

- A minimum number of CDs to sell.

- Some distributors want you to pay for an ad in their catalog or monthly newsletters. This payment may be taken out of one of your invoices, or you might have to pay it up front.

♫ FAST FACT

During the 1980s and early 1990s, a CBS subsidiary, CBS Associated Records, signed artists such as Ozzy Osbourne, The Fabulous Thunderbirds, Electric Light Orchestra, Joan Jett, and Henry Lee Summer.

Bringing in the money

Distributors don't pay you right away when they buy your records. They take your records on consignment or use a purchase order (PO), a document asking for things to be supplied and promising payment. Then, they put your record in retail stores, also on a consignment basis. The distributor will collect payment from the record stores for any records that have been sold. Eventually, you'll get paid from that too. Several months may pass from the time you deliver a shipment of CDs to a distributor until you get payment for it. If it takes a long time, a written letter reminding the company about payments will help.

Distributors usually take your CDs knowing they don't have to pay for around 60 to 120 days. Most details like this can be changed if both sides agree. When the 60 or 120 days have passed, the distributor will not necessarily pay the full amount owed. It will pay only for the number of CDs actually in retail stores, not for the CDs still sitting in its warehouse.

Record stores eventually return all damaged or unsold records to the distributor, who gives them back to the label. If the distributor has already paid the label for those unsold CDs, it could be hard to get any money back. Just so they don't get burned by a big loss, a distributor holds back 15 to 20 percent of the money owed on an invoice until all the records in retail stores have either been paid for or returned. Sometimes, a distributor won't pay until all the records are sold or until it gets a consignment of new records to sell from the record label. This practice is called open invoice.

TIP: How many CDs to consign? As few as possible!

Most distributors have a minimum number of CDs or vinyls you can put on consignment with them. Don't push them to take a larger order — remember, you won't be paid for those CDs until they are sold. If the distributor takes more CDs than it can place in record stores, the rest of them will sit gathering dust for months in a warehouse. You can always give them more CDs when they get close to selling out.

CHAPTER 9

Promotion and Marketing

Successful people in the music industry do two things: make good music and make money by selling that music. After a great artist works at a great recording studio on a great song directed by a great producer and mixed by a great sound engineer, it is time to get out there and sell the music!

You have probably already thought about who will buy your music and how you will reach them. A marketing plan sets out these goals in writing and lists the steps you will take to reach them. You need to make a budget and create a schedule of what will happen when to realize your goals. You can also use it to measure your progress and as a guide to keep you on track.

Marketing music is different from marketing anything else you see in a store. You will succeed when you connect with the emotions, hopes, dreams, and desires of your target audience. Success in the music industry is always changing—media gives you the ability to reach millions of potential fans who will propel you to success in just a few days or weeks, but who are always moving on to something new. You have to adapt quickly to new things while finding ways to keep the interest of loyal fans. Be creative and, at the same time, learn from others and their tried-and-true methods that bring real results.

It's a challenge to find a way to get publicity that won't blow your budget, find ways to get others to help with the work, and find volunteers among your family members and fans who want to support you. Major labels have the money to launch massive advertising campaigns all over. When you start out, or if you're working with a small record label, you may have to do things differently.

Music has to have publicity. When the publicity stops, the sales stop. Sales can grow every time an artist performs in a club, coffee shop, or theaters; at concerts, parties, and festivals; on tours; and whenever possible, on television, the stage, and in movies. The internet shares some new opportunities, like how an artist can stream videos of his or her performances 24 hours a day to anywhere in the world, and social networks where music fans recommend artists to each other.

LEARNING ABOUT YOUR TARGET MARKET

Who do you picture buying this music? Think about the fans—the people who make up your target market. You probably already know something about the people who enjoy the music you want to sell. Look around at the people who come to performances, and write down everything you see: their ages, how they dress, and the different places where they come to hear the music.

You can make up a simple survey with questions about gender, age group, town or city of residence, job or school, favorite genres of music, favorite foods and beverages, favorite music and social networking websites, and how people listen to music (MP3 player, computer, iPhone, stereo system, boombox, car stereo). Make the survey easy to complete by using check-boxes, but leave a few blanks to fill in. Ask how the person heard about this show, and where and how often he or she goes to hear live music. Finally, ask the person to sign up for your email list or newsletter. Leave space at the end for comments. Ask people to fill out the survey as they go in or out of the concert. Thank them with a giveaway, a coupon for free food or drinks, or a free ticket to an upcoming show. Be sure to hand out a schedule of your upcoming performances, a one-sheet, or a flier about your new album as they leave.

♫ FAST FACT

Bing Crosby's "Merry Christmas" was one of the top-selling vinyl albums in 2016 (**www.businessinsider.com**).

Study the surveys and pay attention to what you find. You may discover some surprises—for example, that your fans are older or younger than you thought, or that a rough-looking audience in a club is actually composed of computer programmers and other professionals. A local crowd might not be local after all; people may be driving an hour or two from other towns and cities to come and hear the music.

Don't forget about potential fans who aren't showing up in your live audiences. High school students and underage young people can't get into bars and clubs, but they are a large fan base for many types of music. Release a single or put some free music on your website, and use website analytics — get help if you need to on this — to see exactly where your music is being downloaded or listened to.

Some types of American music, such as hip-hop and rap, are popular overseas. In 2015, a 0.5% increase in revenue from all North American music sales ($4.89 billion total) happened, but statistics also showed $15 billion in international sales that year, driven largely by digital downloads. You could randomly find out that you have a lot of fans in Brazil or the Czech Republic, and then you'll know that you need to market with online advertising or an internet promotion in that region and maybe a tour.

CREATING A MARKETING PLAN

Chat with everyone you know: your producer, recording engineer, studio owner, DJs, promoters, and other artists, and also friends and family. Write down every idea about marketing that they have, no matter how crazy it sounds. Review and add to the list from time to time.

Think about what you know of your fans to come up with obvious strategies for marketing your music. If they go to certain clubs and venues, get to know the owners and DJs, give them promotional CDs to play, and try to schedule live performances there. Look for the same kind of clubs in the area. If your fans listen to a local radio station, try to get radio play, get a live interview with your artist, and look for other radio stations nearby. If people first heard about the band on Facebook, step up your social media game by posting more videos of live performances.

Look around at what other artists who play the same music are doing. Look at their touring schedules, venues, websites, social networking sites, music videos, free downloads, and the merchandise they sell. Look them up on Google, Bing, or Yahoo! to see what kind of internet ads they run and what is being said about them in the news. What works for others might work for you. Focus, especially at the beginning of your career, on personal relationships and word-of-mouth methods for letting people know how awesome your music is.

It's all in the details

You have lots of ideas. Now, choose what will work for you and for your budget. What activities will bring the greatest results? Which of those is most important? When you don't have endless money, time, or staff, you might have to forget some activities so you can do other activities well.

Pick a start date for each activity. Book concerts and be active on social media right away; think about when you will send out press for each new CD or when you will put up posters before a concert. Make a list of the materials you will need, steps for each activity, and how much it will cost and how long it will take to do. Make a checklist from this; it will keep you organized now, and make your planning easier in the future when you do an event similar to this one.

When you spend money, check your budget, and make changes if needed. When you get quotes and when you pay other people, update your budget to see if you are on track.

DON'T FORGET THE SMALL STUFF!

Think of every little detail when planning! For example, if you want to send out press kits on a certain date, you need to schedule a photography session, have someone write press releases, buy folders, make a list of where you're sending them kits, and stuff the envelopes (or put together an email press release) before that date. Posters have to be designed, printed, and shipped before the distribution date. All the artist's performances should be on the calendar — and their publicity events. Don't leave anything out!

You may need a copy of your marketing plan when you approach a distributor, a venue for concerts, or a store owner. A professional-looking marketing plan shows that you know what you are doing and that you are working hard!

ALTERNATIVE MARKETING

Some independent labels and artists use creative grassroots (individual-level) marketing that works so well it is now being used by major labels and entertainment companies. Social media boosts music sales and gets more people to concerts. Street teams hand out fliers, stickers, or free music to people on the street or at other concerts and events; wear your T-shirts and walk around at music festivals and concert venues; put up posters; and visit local music stores with one-sheets to talk up an upcoming performance. At concerts, they can see merchandise and CDs, and help with the crowds. Give the members of your street team free music to hand out to their friends and acquaintances. Start with asking friends and family to help you, then you can move on to actually hiring and paying your street team members.

Remember: You don't just want to sell thousands of copies of a single song, but you want to create a reputation and an image, so that they want to buy concert tickets and future albums. Some things you try might not make tons of sales, but they will help people know you name.

SWAG

In the music industry, swag (Stuff We Always Get) is what we call giveaway items with the band or label's name and URL printed on them. Pens, bottle openers, bags, stickers, posters, transparencies for car windows, T-shirts, and CDs or flash drives with free music can be handed out to increase attention for your artist. Besides concerts, you can give these to stores that sell your music and give the stores free music and free event tickets if they hand them out.

Be creative! Have concerts in bookstores, libraries, museums, and churches; at schools and on college campuses; at festivals, conventions, and music conferences; public parks; private parties; and at mall and store openings. Have a charity fundraiser for a good cause, donate the proceeds from ticket sales, and sell CDs at the event. People who see your artist at these events will go home and look up you up online.

♫ FAST FACT

WEA — soon to become Warner Music Group — was instrumental in the U.S. success of Fleetwood Mac and the pioneer heavy metal bands Led Zeppelin, Black Sabbath, and Deep Purple. Alice Cooper, Montrose, and Van Halen were among the first U.S. metal bands to sign with the label.

LIVE PERFORMANCES

You want live performances to sell music and grow a fan base, but it can be hard for a new artist to get gigs. Start locally, where the artist may already have a reputation in the music scene. Make contacts with clubs and other places in the area that usually have the same kind of artists.

A live performance will bring customers, which makes the venue money by selling drinks. Offer to perform on a weeknight when the place is quiet. Invite family and friends to come. The owner will be motivated to ask you back if you show you can attract a small crowd. Even if it's free, try to set up a regular night to appear; it will build confidence, skills, and more fans!

Find the venues where bands perform, and ask if they need an act to open for them. If you book a venue for yourself, remember that you will have to pay the rent and do publicity for your performance. You shouldn't have to pay anything if another artist asks you to open for them.

When the band performs, tell other venues, promoters, and booking agents so they can come and listen. You never know when you'll get your next booking!

Don't focus on making money at first. The important thing is to be noticed by your audience and to build up a fan base. Some arrangements pay you the same no matter how many people show up. Door split deals let the artist have part of the money people paid for admission. You might not earn any money from some shows and might even end up paying out of your own pocket. It doesn't matter. If someone lets you perform, be grateful and make the most of every opportunity. When you have a good audience at one venue, look for similar clubs. Who knows? They may already have heard about you and would be willing to give you a try.

Always show up on time and ready to perform for every booking. Be professional, no matter what the venue. Keep your website and social media sites up to date with all the details of performances coming up. Get your concerts noticed in events calendars, posters on bulletin boards, and newspaper ads. Put up fliers in local music stores and book stores.

PUBLICITY

You want public attention for your artists and your label. Remember: A positive newspaper article or review is awesome, but people see it for only a short time. There always needs to be new ways to get people interest in the artists and the music. If you can afford it, hire a publicist to make press releases, give stories to newspapers and magazines, and take care of your public profile. You might be able to hire a recent graduate or a freelancer to work part time for you.

There are many ways to get free publicity. Look at all kinds of media, magazines, websites, local newspapers, and local radio stations — they might let you share articles and music for review. Create a press kit to send out, and follow up with press releases when something exciting comes up. It is much easier to create a buzz around a specific event, such as an upcoming concert, a new release, or when something personal (and positive) happens in the artist's life — an awards show, a wedding, and so on.

Make a list of journalists, music critics, writers, radio hosts, and PR representatives, and send them invitations to the live performances. Ask if the person wants to be added to your guest list. If someone from the media comes to a concert, be sure to greet him or her personally. Send out holiday cards, free music — and sometimes small presents are nice, too!

Local newspapers, radio shows, and websites are always looking for events to add to their community calendars. This can be a great way to find free publicity.

Press kits and promo packages

Question: *What goes in a press kit?*
Answer: *Pictures, press clippings, and background information that can be put together and sent out at a moment's notice whenever someone asks for information.*

Hire a good professional photographer to do a photo shoot with the artist. You want top-quality photos that show the right image and personality. Newspapers and magazines like to publish images along with their stories; if you supply some amazing photos, they will be more likely to take notice of you.

Start collecting press clippings, reviews, quotes from radio interviews, and any news videos about the band. Make a promo package with a photo, short bio or one-sheet, and the press clippings. Keep adding updates to the promo package. Your press kit should include your contact information, a short history of the label, the artists' promo packages, a press release with information about an upcoming event or release of an album, and important news articles.

Don't hand out something large or bulky. Journalists don't want to search through stacks of papers. A great idea is to use a cardboard folder with two pockets. You can have a cardboard folder printed with the label logo and the artists' names, or use a plain folder with a printed adhesive label. Always include a business card.

If you are sending your press kit or promo package by email, copy and paste the information into the email and provide a link to your website. Don't attach anything to the email—it might not get through the company's spam filter, and journalists are not likely to open attachments anyway. After emailing, follow up with a personal phone call; otherwise, you have no assurance that the journalist saw it.

In the media section on your website, you can post photos, your press kit and promo package, and press releases. If there are things you don't want everyone in the world to see, create a special login, and give out the password only to certain people. A media section lets anyone who is interested in your label get information without having to contact you.

Submitting your CD for review

Music reviewers working for magazines, newspapers, and the internet see many records, so you need to make your submission stand out. The best way to do this is to contact the reviewer personally and ask how you can send a submission for review. Follow those instructions. Send a CD, the artist's one-sheet, and a press release about the album. Don't forget to write a personal note thanking the reviewer for his or her time. Start with reviewers who write for local newspapers or genre magazines. A regional newspaper might be interested in a local artist. A good local review might get picked up by other media and lead to further reviews, or show up online when people are looking for information on your artist.

Advertising

A newspaper or magazine article fades from interest quickly. You need to be in the media all the time, and that can only happen through paid advertising. Find places to run your ads where they will be successful. Study what advertising has been done by other artists and what publications run their ads.

A full-page ad can be expensive, but there are many ways to save money. Run a half-page or a quarter-page ad instead. Your ad will be on display longer in a monthly or bi-monthly magazine than in a weekly one. Ads in some specialty magazines continue to bring results for months after publication. You might be able to get a record store to trade advertising for free music. You can also offer to perform in a store if it will pay to advertise you. Double up on your ads by sharing a tour schedule and a new release in the same ad.

PLANNING PUBLICITY AROUND A NEW RELEASE

Publicity works best when it is focused on one event, like a new release or a concert tour. A time limit gives fans a sense of excitement — think of the hundreds of people camping out to attend a theater's first showing of a new *Star Wars*, *Lord of the Rings*, or *Twilight* movie, even though it is having "first showings" in many other places. When a new CD is released, you can send out press releases, invite media and fans to listen at a special event, put posters up in music stores, and advertise on the internet.

♫ **FAST FACT**

WEA — the company that would become Warner Music Group — began distributing a number of successful independent labels in the 1980s.

This takes a lot of planning. First, make sure that your CD will be in your hands, ready to sell, on the release date. You're wasting time and money if you book a venue, invite hundreds of guests, pay for food and drinks, and then don't have CDs to sell at your launch party. Schedule advertising, print posters, and deliver CDs to retail stores. Magazines might need several months before they can print an article. Stay on schedule with every detail. If something is not ready by the due date, change the plans.

New CDs need launch parties. When looking for a venue, keep in mind that a local place might be willing to host your party for free if your artist performs afterward for regular patrons. Invite everyone on your contact list: media, promoters, club owners, DJs, retailers, other musicians, family, and friends. Follow up with a phone call to confirm they will attend; nothing is worse than a half-empty room at a media event. Have food and drinks. At a typical launch party, the entire album is played for the guests over the sound system, followed by a live performance. Sell CDs, hand out one-sheets, and get email addresses. For a new artist, the launch party may be the first chance to sell a lot of CDs.

The release needs to happen at the right time. Many people buy CDs during November and December when they're shopping for the holidays. The big names launch their music at that time to get high sales. If you launch a CD during a quieter season, you'll have a better chance of being noticed.

SOCIAL MEDIA (IT'S REALLY FOR EVERYONE)

From big artists to brand new labels, almost everyone in the music industry now relies on social media to drive sales of music downloads and CDs, and to boost ticket sales and attendance at events. People use websites, blogs, email, instant messaging, forums, video, or chat rooms. You know Facebook and Instagram and Twitter, with their hundreds of millions of members, but there are thousands of smaller sites focused on specific interests or age groups. Many allow users to share favorite music, videos, and photos with the click of a button.

When people use social media, they feel in control of their internet experiences. They can make their own connections with friends and contacts through websites with music, photos, and more. The internet is deeply engaging, and, for some people, even addictive. Members of some online communities that are fiercely loyal to a celebrity, artist, or cause will give their time, money, and influence to supporting them.

If you catch the attention of enough people, they will tell their friends, who tell their friends, and your fame will quickly spread across nations and continents. This phenomenon, called viral marketing, can be extremely effective, but it doesn't happen by chance. Social networking, like any public relations effort, requires hours of work, regular updates, constant monitoring, and ongoing research into the latest trends and technologies. You or your artist may have the know-how and interest to do this work yourselves; if not, pay someone else to do it for you. Social networking is an opportunity that you can't neglect. There are companies who do only do social media for musicians, or you can hire a local fan or college student to take care of your social networks.

One awesome thing about social media: It's free. Although anyone can make a profile on a social networking site, link it to your website, post a video of a concert, and tell your friends, social media marketing is actually complex. You want to focus on reaching a specific audience. Everyone does not use social networking in the same way. Think about who your fans are—their ages, gender, and musical interests. Sign up as a "follower" on the social networks of artists like yours and observe how they promote themselves, then try it yourself.

Make a profile for your artist or label on social networking sites and on music websites. Each site has profile pages, and many allow you to share photos, videos, streaming music or music downloads. Link these profiles to your official website. Many social networking sites have widgets—small graphic symbols that you can place on your websites, blogs, and articles to link readers to your profile page in that social network. For example, a Twitter widget on your official website lets fans sign up to follow you on Twitter, or to tweet their friends about you. Some sites have features that let you sell your CDs and downloads directly; others link to a sales page like Amazon.com or iTunes.

♫ FAST FACT

If you signed a contract with an online distributor, check the contract for any rules about selling your music independently.

Once you've made profiles on the social media sites, here are some ways to be a boss on the internet:

- Link to your social network profiles. Put a widget somewhere on each page, or a link saying something like, "Follow me on Twitter."

- Use social bookmarking to help more people see your site. Social bookmarking means making playlists or lists of favorite websites that can be shared with friends online. It also includes tagging to show that the reader "likes" or "recommends" you to others. Example: Pandora now shares individuals' playlists with their Facebook friends.

- Make and share music videos and photos on Flickr and YouTube. Upload film clips from recent concerts, live interviews, rehearsals, jam sessions, and photo shoots. Keeping it fresh will keep fans coming back for more.

- Promote songs through your profile on social networking and music sites with links to your home page and a sales page.

- Use Twitter to send out news for your fans, such as a concert or a new song or videos available on the internet.

- Invite fans to sign up for your email list for announcements and special offers.

You can't expect your fans to do all the work for you. Social networking is cool because it's different for everyone; every person feels he or she is giving something and receiving individual attention. Communication is important. Your website and social media should all connect. The artist, or someone on your staff, must answer emails and messages quickly. Find ways to reward fans who participate in your social networks with invitations to spontaneous performances or meet-and-greet opportunities after concerts, exclusive access to video clips, and free music.

Internet users like to see something new once or twice a week. Someone on your team should be always updating blogs, uploading video clips of recent performances, posting news, and dropping hints about new songs and upcoming releases. Make the fans feel like they are "in the know."

♫ FAST FACT

Among EMI's artists during the 1930s and 1940s were Arturo Toscanini, Sir Edward Elgar, and Otto Klemperer.

Don't forget that you're competing with thousands of other labels and artists for fans' attention. In 2012, Facebook had over 500,000 musician pages. The quality of your music alone will not be enough to make you stand out. Your marketing, and your ability to expand your fan base by coming up with new music and new ideas, will make the difference.

MUSIC WEBSITES THAT INTERACT WITH SOCIAL NETWORKING MEDIA

Amazon (www.amazon.com)
If you have exclusive rights to your CDs, you can sell your CDs on Amazon.com by producing them on-demand through CreateSpace (**www.createspace.com**) or selling physical inventory on consignment through Amazon Advantage (you will have to send enough copies of your CD to meet customer demand for several weeks). In order to sell MP3 files as downloads on Amazon, you must go through one of these distributors:

- CD Baby (**www.cdbaby.com**)
- Createspace (**www.createspace.com**)
- ELDistribution (**www.e1distribution.com**)
- INgrooves (**www.ingrooves.com**)
- Iris Distribution (**www.irisdistribution.com**)
- Red Eye (**www.redeyeusa.com**)
- The Orchard (**www.theorchard.com**)
- Tunecore (**www.tunecore.com**)
- Virtual Label (**www.virtuallabel.biz**)

Amazon allows artists and labels to create online artist stores for free. Photos, artwork, music and content to enhance these sites can be uploaded through Artist Central (**https://artistcentral.amazon.com**).

Bandcamp (http://bandcamp.com)

Bandcamp allows you to get your music out for free, charge a set price for it, or let fans name their own price, with the minimum set by you. You can sell both physical merchandise and digital music from Bandcamp, and create combo packages like a vinyl record, poster, and download bundle where fans get the digital files immediately and the merchandise in the mail. And hey — each account gets 200 free downloads to give away to fans each month.

Jango Music Network (www.jango.com)

Jango is an ad-funded social music service that lets listeners create and share custom radio stations. Its unique "Jango Airplay" music promotion service gives emerging artists guaranteed airplay as similar artists alongside the popular artists chosen by listeners. Packages start at as little as $10 for 250 plays.

Last.fm (www.last.fm)

Last.fm is a music recommendation service that delivers personalized recommendations to every one of its listeners every day. It maintains online communities, encourages social tagging, and allows listeners to connect their playlists through Twitter. It gives you exposure to new fans. You can give your listeners free downloads, stream your music, or sell downloads.

MySpace Music (www.myspace.com/music/artisthq)

Myspace Music is known for its artist profile pages and playlist features. The site tracks the most popular music — kind of like *Billboard charts* — and lets users see music that is popular in other countries. You can sell music on MySpace either through an online distributor or by placing a link to another sales page on your profile.

Pandora (www.pandora.com)

Pandora is an ad-funded internet music recommendation service based on the Music Genome Project®, a database built from over eight years of analysis by a trained team of music scientists using up to 400 distinct musical characteristics. The database spans everything from new releases to Renaissance and Classical music. Listeners can build playlists based on their favorite music. The Music Genome Project is continually updated with the latest releases, emerging artists, and an ever-growing collection of songs. If you have music you want them to consider using, email suggest-music@pandora.com.

ReverbNation (www.reverbnation.com)

Here you can make a profile and use free viral marketing tools for MySpace, Facebook, Twitter, blogs, and websites. Develop a mailing list and send email newsletters with the free version of FanReach™, the email system more than 40,000 artists use.

RootMusic (www.rootmusic.com)

A RootMusic BandPage™ lets fans listen to new tracks while reading more about your artist and looking at your upcoming event schedule. Tracks play through a special Facebook-share enabled SoundCloud music player. Fans can purchase or download music through links on SoundCloud. Fans can easily share and send music through their Facebook networks.

SoundCloud (www.soundcloud.com)

SoundCloud lets artists upload or record originally created sounds and share them via social networking sites, along with visuals. Timed comments let friends and fans give feedback at specific moments throughout the music.

thesixtyone.com (www.thesixtyone.com)

On thesixtyone, artists can sign up to sell songs and merchandise directly to fans. Artists make at least $7 per album and are paid every 30 days.

YouTube (www.youtube.com)

Artists can create a profile and upload music videos, which fans share through social media. A link on the profile can connect the listener to a sales page.

CASE STUDY: DANIEL ENNIS

Student, University of Florida

Communication Is the Key

At the University of Florida, Ennis is double majoring in advertising and English.

I have played in several bands over the last seven years, and before coming to college, I used to set up shows for other musicians to play too. We recorded a lot of music in those bands but didn't have much interest in making money from it. We mostly just ended up handing CDs out at cost or giving free downloads to people. We didn't make money, but we had a reputation in our hometown.

With websites such as Bandcamp, MySpace, Facebook, and other social media channels, music can be spread with the click of a button. This can be advantageous for do-it-yourself types because relatively unknown bands can easily attract fans all over the world, but at the same time, it's detrimental to the record label system that has been in place since music has been recorded. Anybody can download anything. Social media and the internet perpetuate this spread of information and give opportunities to bands that wouldn't ordinarily get attention. At the same time, the notoriety of bands that become known on e-zine and music community websites such as Pitchfork Media (**http://pitchfork.com**) or Stereogum (**www.stereogum.com**) has a shorter shelf-life. Bands come and go as frequently as the seasons, and trends in styles come and go at the same time. It's a very interesting time, with a lot of opportunity for the early adapters that are willing to take a little risk and play the game.

If you have a DIY label, one of the biggest difficulties is creating interest. If the music is good enough, then it will speak for itself, so to speak. But it's not always that easy. When the label promotes its artists through shows to create a grassroots feel, while at the same time utilizing new forms of social media such as YouTube, it is easier for the listener to participate in generating interest, which makes it easier for the DIY label to exist.

Communication with potential fans is also a key. Communication, always seeming "new" and in the moment, always creating new things, or giving the impression that new things are always coming out is really important. But at the same time, you don't want to saturate your audience with too much all at the same time. If the band can find the right balance between saturation and silence, they are likely to be able to get interest and notoriety enough to build a network of fans that come back for more.

The best way to succeed on Twitter is to be interactive. If you're talking a lot, responding quickly to anyone's retweets and mentions, they're more likely to have a conversation with you. Conversation is a big way to get attention that can then promote music.

Social media is moving very fast all the time that it's hard to predict which direction will be next. I would like to be able to say that Facebook will be around forever, but I know that's not true — not by a long shot. Commercialization takes away the appeal of many sites such as Twitter, Facebook, and Tumblr, so people are more likely to abandon one social medium in search for another that doesn't disrupt their day-to-day socializing as much.

People will want to keep finding ways to communicate on the internet and find new ways to interact so they can find new music (and other things such as news and videos). Still, it's hard to say what's next. Maybe Xanga will make a revival, but for the sake of people on the internet everywhere, I hope it doesn't. (Xanga was notorious for illegal file sharing and pornography.)

MUSIC VIDEOS

The International Federation of the Phonographic Industry says that in 2016, a major label typically spends from $50,000 to $3,000,000 to produce a package of three videos for a new artist breaking in a major market. These videos are huge deals that are shown on television and sold on their own as product.

♫ FAST FACT

When the distributor of what would become Warner Music Group was unable to keep up with the demand for newly emerging Grateful Dead albums, the company established an in-house distribution arm.

For independent labels, the role of music videos has changed. Instead of seeing an artist for the first time in a music video on television, most potential fans are exposed to a new artist online through video clips. Fans search for videos of the artists they want to see. The photographic quality of the video is no longer as important because it will probably be viewed on a computer screen or even a phone. With so many video clips available, it is important to have videos that are interesting and get the viewer involved with the artist.

With today's digital cameras and editing software, it is possible to make your own good-quality videos. Fans like variety; they like to see different versions of individual songs and videos of live performances. Each time you upload a new video, your fans will share it with others, increasing your exposure and the traffic to your websites. You can also make DVDs of your lower-quality videos to hand out to fans at concerts and give away in record stores.

CONCLUSION

What Does the Future Hold?

Technology has changed so much over the last decade, and that has changed the music industry. Old business models have been destroyed, making people really worry whether the recording industry can survive. An artist can get fans all over the world faster and easier than ever before, but the money coming in from music sales is declining. Can record labels afford to continue investing in new artists? In a 2016 report, the International Federation of the Phonographic Industry (IFPI) said the music industry as a whole spends $4.3 billion annually in musical talent. Almost 30 percent of its total revenue is invested in A&R and marketing. The music business is risky; if you're lucky, one in five or even only one in ten will be successful. The money earned by record companies is used to develop new artists. If record companies can't make enough profit, new artists will never have a chance.

Another serious threat to the music industry is digital piracy through illegal file-and- pirating music. Harris Interactive reports that 14 percent of the music obtained online in the U.K. during 2010 was unlicensed. The IFPI report also cites a study from Sweden that says that physical music sales would be 72 percent higher and digital music 131 higher percent if piracy did not exist. People involved in all parts of the music industry want consumers to know about the need to pay for music in order to support artists.

Major record labels have been adapting to face these challenges by trying to increase revenue from other sources such as live performances, merchandise sales, and licensing. There is no guarantee this will compensate for the decline in revenue from record sales; according to Pollstar, during 2015, box office sales of the world's top Top 100 Worldwide Tours made a total of $4.71 billion. That is up 11 percent over 2014 but less than the record $5 billion set in 2013. These up and down numbers could be a temporary trend because of people worrying over the economy, or a permanent shift in the way audiences enjoy music.

Some believe that allowing free music on the internet actually supports record sales by helping an artist become well known so that fans ultimately want to purchase studio-quality CDs and downloads. They want to try out new business models where fans are happy to pay for personalized music experiences by using subscription services, interactive devices, and buying merchandise and event tickets. Others look ahead to free music everything supported by ads.

It is hard to guess how audiences will be listening to their music in five years. One thing is certain: those who can be flexible enough to try new ideas, stay on a budget, find their loyal fans, while using creative marketing, will have the most success in the music industry.

PHOTO CREDITS

These photos require special attribution.

Introduction
Page 14: Debby Wong.

Chapter 4
Page 72: Julija Sh.
Page 84: WDnet Studio.

Chapter 5
Page 116: Peter Gudella.

GLOSSARY

360 (or multiple rights) deals: An increasingly popular deal that a major record label signs with an artist that allows them to get part of the earnings from all of a band's activities—not just record sales.

Á la carte: The sale of individual songs; the buyer picks and chooses only the songs he or she likes from an album.

Advance: The payment that some record label offer artists when they sign the contract before any music has been produced or sold. The company later gets the money from the sales of the record.

Catalog number: An arrangement of three letters followed by three numbers—such as "XYZ123"—assigned to each record.

Cleans: CDs sold in stores, as opposed to promotional CD.

Click track: Essentially, a metronome—cues that help synchronize a recording.

Co-publishing agreement: The artist's publishing company owning the copyrights, and then giving part of those rights to the label's publishing company.

Copyright: Legal protection as promised in the U.S. Constitution and given by law for original work.

Cover: Another band or musician performing and recording the work or song of a different band or musician, such as Michael Bublé performing Bing Crosby's music.

Cross-collateralization: An artist agreeing to apply some of his or her mechanical royalties to recording expenses.

Force majeure: Literally, "superior force." It is a clause that protects the label in case something happens beyond its control—a natural disaster, fire, accident, etc.

Genre: A certain type or kind of a thing. In music, different genres include hip-hop, jazz, R&B, rock 'n' roll, pop, etc.

Glass master: A circular glass block about 240 mm in diameter with a special chemical coating that is used to replicate CDs since the information from the master recording is engraved on the face of the glass master.

Indemnity clause: A clause that means the artist has to pay if the record label is sued because of the artist's work.

Leaving member option: The record label signing one artist to a solo record deal in case the artist wants to leave a band to record a solo album; the contract in this case will be similar to the one signed by the group as a whole.

License: A license gives permission to use a song; there are many different kinds of licenses for many different kinds of uses.

Marketing plan: A document that sets out in writing a person's or company's goals about who will buy the product and how to reach those customers.

Master use license: A license for the recorded version of a song. To get this, a company also needs a mechanical license.

Mechanical license: A license that gives a record label permission to copy a song and distribute it.

Mechanical royalties: Royalties collected on the use of copyrighted, published material.

Mixing: Blending together all of the different versions of the song that were recorded in the studio to create the best possible version.

One-stops: Subdistributors that wholesale a wide selection of CDs, movies, games, and other media to smaller independent stores.

Open invoice: A distributor not paying until all the records are sold or until it gets a consignment of new records to sell from the record label.

Payola: A company or organization paying radio stations and disc jockeys to play the songs of various artists; this is an illegal practice.

Performance royalties: Royalties earned when a song is played on the radio.

Purchase order: A document asking for things to be supplied and promising payment.

Recoupable: Expense that are paid first by the record label and then paid back by the artist through royalties.

Sampled record: A record that takes part of one recording—a sample—and reuses it in another recording.

Side artist agreement: A record label agreeing that one of its artists can do backup work for another artist.

Street teams: Groups of people working for a band or organization that hand out fliers, stickers, and free music to people on the street at concerts and other events; wear T-shirts and walk around at music festivals and concert venues; put up posters; and visit local music stores with one-sheets to talk up an upcoming performance. At concerts, they can see merchandise and CDs, and help with the crowds.

Suspension: A suspension of a contract means there is a problem that needs to be fixed by a certain time.

Swag: Short for Stuff We Always Get. Giveaway items with the band or label's name and URL printed on them.

Synchronization license: A license that allows a video to be shown on TV or in a movie.

Termination: A termination of a contract means that the whole deal is off.

Territory: The term for place where a contract binds the signers. For instance, if a record label was only going to be able to sell a musician's music in the U.S., the U.S. would be the territory. Generally, however, in music contracts the territory is "the world."

Trademark: A word, phrase, symbol, or design—or some combination of these—that sets a person, company, etc. apart from others.

Untethered file: All files that a person can listen to without being connected to the internet.

Videogram license: A license that allows an organization to make a music video.

Warranty: An artist's promise to the label that nothing will happen that could sabotage the recording.

Widget: Small graphic symbols that placed on a website, blog, or in articles to link readers to a profile page in that social network. Common widgets include Twitter, Facebook, etc.

BIBLIOGRAPHY

Christman, Ed. "BMG's Purchase of Bug Music Finds It Closing in on Majors." Billboard.com. 2011. **billboard.com/biz/articles/news/publishing/1169240/bmgs-purchase-of-bug-music-finds-it-closing-in-on-majors.**

Copyright.gov. "Copyright in General." **http://www.copyright.gov/help/faq/faq-general.html#what.**

Hagerty, Jim. "How to Write a Music Contract." eHow. **http://www.ehow.com/how_8205068_make-recording-contract.html.**

Harry Fox Agency. "Statutory Royalty Rates." 2013. **https://secure.harryfox.com/public/StatutoryReports.jsp.**

Herzfeld, Oliver. "Are Your Emails Enforceable Contracts?" Forbes. 2013. **http://www.forbes.com/sites/oliverherzfeld/2013/12/09/are-your-emails-enforceable-contracts/#6742a877383c.**

Holofcener, Adam. "The Right to Terminate: A Musician's Guide to Copyright Reversion." Future of Music Coalition. 2012. **http://futureofmusic.org/article/fact-sheet/right-terminate-musicians%E2%80%99-guide-copyright-reversion.**

IFPI. "Digital Music Report." 2011. http://proxy.siteo.com.s3.amazonaws
.com/disqueenfrance.siteo.com/file/9ifpidigitalmusicreport2011
.pdf.

IFPI. "Investing in Music." http://www.ifpi.org/how-record-labels
-invest.php.

IFPI. "IPFI Publishes Digital Music Report 2015." 2015. http://www
.ifpi.org/news/Global-digital-music-revenues-match-physical
-format-sales-for-first-time.

Ingham, Tim. "BMG Revenues Top $200M in H1 2016, With an 18%
Profit Margin." Music Business Worldwide. 2016. http://www.mu-
sicbusinessworldwide.com/
bmg-revenues-top-200m-in-h1-2016-with-an-18-profit-margin.

"Legal Issues Involved in the Music Industry." Lawyers for the Creative
Arts. 2005. http://www.law-arts.org/pdf/Legal_Issues_in_the_Music
_Industry.pdf.

Legal Language Services. "How Long Copyright Protection Endures." 2016.
http://www.legallanguage.com/resources/copyright/copyright
-protection-endurance/.

Reverbnation.com "Email and Social Marketing." 2016. http://www
.reverbnation.com/main/overview_artist?feature=fanreach.

Moyer, Justin M. "Paul McCartney Takes Battle for Beatles Songs to Copyright Office." Washington Post. 2016. https://www.washingtonpost
.com/news/morning-mix/wp/2016/03/22/paul-mccartney-takes
-battle-for-beatles-songs-to-copyright-office/

Smith, Ethan. "Jackson Estate Steers to Next Challenge: Loan Refinanc-
ing." The Wall Street Journal. 2010. http://online.wsj.com/article/SB
10001424052748703438604575315364195884770.html.

Steele, Robert. "If You Think Piracy Is Decreasing, You Haven't Looked at the Data." Digital Music News. **http://www.digitalmusicnews .com/2015/07/16/if-you-think-piracy-is-decreasing-you-havent -looked-at-the-data-2**.

USATODAY.com "Country Music Brings Out Big Guns for Peak Sales Season." 2010. **http://usatoday30.usatoday.com/life/music/news/ 2010-09-15-countryglut15_ST_N.htm**.

Vertesi, Campbell. "How to Cite a Music CD." eHow. **http://www.ehow .com/how_6687327_cite-cd-recording.html**.

Vincent, James. "Digital Music Revenue Overtakes CD Sales for the First Time Globally." TheVerge.com. 2015. **http://www.theverge. com/2015/4/15/8419567/digital-physical-music-sales-overtake -globally**.

INDEX

ABOUT THE AUTHOR

Born in Colorado, Angela Erickson married a handsome Texan and spent 10 years living down in the South before recently moving back to her home state. She and her husband Kyle have four kids—three girls and a boy. She has worn many "career" hats over the years, including youth ministry director, middle school teacher, full-time mama, marketing assistant for a waterpark, and freelance writer. Angela loves reading, writing, music, running, and spending time with family and friends. She is borderline addicted to puttering around on ancestry.com, and she is also an enthusiastic anglophile.